Northwest
Native Harvest

Text and Illustrations
by Carol Batdorf

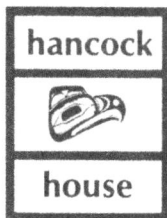

hancock
house

ISBN-10:   0-88839-245-1
ISBN-13:   978-0-88839-245-9
Copyright © 1990 Carol Batdorf

2018 Reprint

Cataloging in Publication Data

Batdorf, Carol, 1919-

Northwest Native Harvest

Includes bibliographical references. **ISBN** 0-88839-245-1

1. Coast Salish Indians - Food.   I. Title

E99.S21B381990   641'.089'979   C90-091107-7

The material in this book was first published by (the author for and in cooperation with) the Whatcom Museum of History and Art, Bellingham, WA, in 1980.
This edition contains additional material.

Printed in the United States

Published simultaneously in Canada and the United States by

hancock

house

H A N C O C K H O U S E P U B L I S H E R S L T D.
19313 Zero Ave., Surrey, B.C. V3Z 9R9
(604) 538-1114 Fax (604) 538-2262

H A N C O C K H O U S E P U B L I S H E R S
#104-4550 Birch Bay-Lynden Rd, Blaine, WA 98230
(800) 938-1114 Fax (800) 983-2262
www.hancockhouse.com sales@hancockhouse.com

This book is dedicated to Angelina Alexander, who spent many hours telling me things that she remembered from a girlhood in which she lived much as her elders had in the "old days."

Foreword

IT WAS MY MOTHER, Angelina Alexander, who first introduced Carol Batdorf to the old Indian ways of getting and preparing food. Carol promised her that she would put the material in a book so that everyone could know something about the old days. I am happy that it has been done and hope that people who read it will understand more about how the old people thought and lived.

ALICE SOLOMAN
Lummi 1980

Contents

Preface

FOR MANY YEARS Indian friends have given me "gifts" of information on the old ways and how things used to be among the Salish people of the Puget Sound. I was fascinated by the tales of elderly women. They told how their mothers and grandmothers labored to gather, prepare, and cook their native food. "It was hard work," they would say. "Women today don't know how to work like that. When it was all done it tasted good. You don't taste food like that any more."

With notebook in hand, I would hastily jot down the descriptions and recipes. Not wanting to interrupt the flow of thought as those venerable ladies reminisced, and not wanting to appear to be writing rather than listening, my notes were sketches of thoughts: part quick drawings, part shorthand. The notes filled boxes and then sat waiting for the day when I could get to them.

That day came, eventually, and I began the task of making sense out of the scribblings and then compiling them into some sort of meaningful form. Since the information came from several Salish groups, I was forced to generalize a bit and gloss over the fact that there were differences in the ways that even close Salish neighbors did things. As much as possible, I tried to include only the information I had been given first hand, but when an obvious discrepancy arose or some vital link was missing, I resorted to other authorities for clarification or the necessary facts.

The results of my efforts are not intended to be a complete study, but rather a glimpse into the ways that the Salish people of the Puget Sound area solved the problem of feeding themselves by utilizing the food that their environment had to offer. I hope that you will find my drawings helpful in finding some of the plants and berries, should you choose to do so, but I recommend that you also consult a good botanical guide for this area. By using this book and a reference work together, you will minimize the chance of finding and preparing an unpalatable or poisonous food.

It is my hope that the information this book contains will generate an interest in, and appreciation of, the Coast Salish culture.

CAROL BATDORF
Bellingham 1990

Introduction

THEY WERE GOURMETS, the Coast Salish Indians. They lived along the shores of Puget Sound, inhabiting the bays and estuaries in the days before the white man came. The sea, the mountains, the forests, the prairies, and the lakes and rivers all poured forth their abundance to them. With the leisure that such plenty provides, the women were able to develop ingenious methods of cookery to nourish and delight those who dined at their fires. Their menus were balanced and varied. Each of the seasons brought a unique contribution of food to the Coast Salish people.

Salmon teemed in the cold water off the people's villages. Halibut, big as rowboats, lay on the sea floor. Cod lurked near the reefs, and snapper, perch, herring, flounder, and dogfish swarmed in untold numbers. Smelt came by the thousands to lay their eggs along the beaches. Sea mammals such as seals, sea lions, porpoises, and otters basked on rocky islets and swam in the open water.

The beaches yielded an incredible amount of shellfish. There were large tasty horse clams, smaller succulent butter clams, cockles often lying atop the sand, and littlenecks just under the surface. Huge Dungeness and smaller rock and spider crabs were found in the seaweed. Octopuses, sea cucumbers, sea urchins, moon snails, whelks, barnacles, and all manner of sea creatures inhabited the rocks and reefs.

For variety, Indian hunters turned to the forests and mountains. There, deer, bear, elk, and mountain goat were taken. The sky, too, gave of its bounty. In the spring and fall the air was filled with migrating ducks and geese.

Berries grew in profusion from the marshland to the mountains. Cranberries were found in the lowland bogs, wild strawberries bloomed in open meadows, and blackberries crowded the sunny spaces while salmonberry and thimbleberry grew under the dense forest cover. Salal and soapberries thrived in the moist salt air, and on up the rivers huckleberries grew taller than a man. Higher, in the mountain meadows, blueberries hung so lush they could be combed from the branches.

Ferns reached a prodigious size in the moist, warm climate. Bracken, sword, lady, and licorice ferns yielded roots that were nourishing and tasty. Wild water lilies, skunk cabbage, and cattails produced fat, starchy roots which were processed into useful staples. There were greens, too, like miner's lettuce, clover, and cow parsnip. Seaweed had its place in the people's diet, in part because of its salt. Wild rice was harvested in the marshy lowlands, and the wapato, or wild potato, was dug in the prairies. To add zest to it all, there was the nodding onion that grew in dry, open spaces.

Indian women, through the centuries, devised creative methods of gathering, preparing, and preserving the food which nature provided. They learned when the edibles were mature and ripe for harvesting, and they developed tools and techniques for the work. They learned which wood to use and which kind of fire best suited their needs. They designed and made their own cooking utensils and equipment from materials available to them.

Their cookery was efficient, wholesome, and nutritious. It is of particular interest with today's emphasis on natural food. It is the aim of this book to give the reader an understanding of Indian cookery—with practical recipes where appropriate—and to explain the close relationship between Indian food and the Northwest Coast Indian culture as a whole.

Food and Culture  1

THE DAILY LIFE of the Coast Salish people revolved around the food cycle. Gathering, preparing, and preserving food was of paramount importance, dictating where the people would be and what they would be doing for nine months. Far from being restrictive, the pursuit of food opened the gates to travel and adventure. Depending on the season, the tribes might be encamped on some island beach, paddling their seagoing canoes across the straits of Puget Sound, or venturing up the rivers into the high country. These experiences added excitement to their lives and formed the basis for colorful stories which were repeated around the winter fires.

The abundance of food found in the Puget Sound area meant that leisure time was available for the development of a dynamic culture. This leisure time opened the avenues for amassing great wealth; wealth that consisted of songs and stories and dances as well as art objects and the necessities of life. A full larder was important as a means of enhancing the social status of families. Those who had the ability to give huge feasts and potlatches were regarded as tribal leaders, enjoying a position of great prestige.

The great winter festivals dealt with such important aspects of the Salish culture as the giving of names, initiation into societies, and exhibiting "spirit power." They demanded great quantities of food to feed the many invited guests, often numbering in the hundreds. The kinds and volume of food offered could either add greatly to the prestige of the host and his extended family or it could embarrass them, leaving them open to ridicule.

The host family was faced with the logistics problem of feeding a hoard of visitors for as long as they chose to stay, perhaps a week or more. Not only must the menu be adequate, but it must also be lavish, giving the impression that food was so plentiful that it could be actually wasted. All of this meant, of course, that the people spent much of their time procuring and processing food, far beyond their own personal needs.

The people felt the deepest respect for those plants and animals that formed their diet. These were an integral part of their culture. They believed that all things had been created to live together in

9

mutual goodwill, sharing and intertwining their lives. They had no wish to injure or to dominate other life forms. They appreciated the unique qualities of each species and looked on them as helpers.

In order to rationalize their need to kill for survival, an elaborate structure of beliefs developed. It was based on two assumptions. First, that all living things were originally created the same, had the ability to communicate with each other, and lived together harmoniously as brothers. Second, that nothing really dies: living things are merely released to return to their ideal state in the spirit world. So it follows that if it is done with respect and according to the proper formalities, killing is not killing at all, but assisting the animal or plant to return to its ancestral home.

An old man, a storyteller, recalls an ancient myth which gives some insight into this belief.

"At one time, long before people and animals assumed the forms they now hold, all things were the same. The great Creator made all the creatures to live together in peace and harmony. They could talk together and looked upon each other as brothers. That was the original creation.

"Then things began to change. The creatures began to quarrel among themselves. Some became selfish and thought only of what was best for them. Others became lazy and wouldn't do their part. Some grew dishonest, and others were unkind. Those who tried to live as the Creator wished were forced to provide for the rest.

"Gha-hals, the Son of the Creator, became concerned about this and so he decided to disguise himself and go about the land, testing each kind of animal. His plan was to change those creatures that had not proved to be successful creations, punishing them for their shortcomings.

"As Gha-hals, or the Changer, journeyed about he saw many disturbing things. He found selfishness and greed and trickery among the creatures. So, bit by bit, he re-created the world. He changed some animals into water creatures, giving them tails and fins and depriving them of the ability to walk on the land. Some he caused to live under the ground, and others to come out only at night, living in the darkness. He changed the bodies of some so that they were suited only for certain tasks, such as the beaver who was made to build dams, and the spider who was told to spin webs. In some cases, he punished wrongdoers by depriving them of body parts, as he did the snake, or by changing their shape, as happened to the weasel.

10

"He deprived animals of the power of speech because of their foolish tongues. He made man to walk upright and to be master of the world, but he instructed him to remember that the animals and birds and fish were his brothers.

"As Gha-hals was making his tour of the world, adding here and there to the creation of his father, and changing things to their present form, he came down a channel to the San Juan Islands. Making his way from island to island, he noticed that they were barren. There was no food on them for the people to eat. So he began to plant various ferns and roots in the ground and to place shellfish on the beaches.

"He planted camas, ferns, and blackberries on Lummi and Vendovi islands. Then he traveled on to Sucia Island where he placed mussels on the rocks. The grateful people named the island Selequem, which means mussels. When Gha-hals reached Patos Island, he found the beaches just right for oysters, so he planted them there. The people then named the island Quailiton, meaning oyster."

The old man paused in his narrative and looked off toward the horizon for a long time. That is the Indian way, to lose one's self in contemplation . . . and it is also the Indian way for the listener to be patient, for eventually, when his spirit has returned, the storyteller will continue. At last, the old man aroused himself and began to speak again.

"That is the creation that we see today," he said. "We only see the changes that Gha-hals made. But someday, if we act as men should and respect all the forms of life which the Creator made . . . once again we will be as brothers. Then we can communicate with the birds and animals and fish, and each 'tribe' will live in its own place. The fish people will live in their villages under the sea, the animals will live as brothers of men and the birds will watch over us all. Everything will be once again as the Creator made it."

The Indians believed that animals and plants could bestow their special abilities upon humans in the form of "gifts," provided certain conditions were met.

Young men, upon reaching puberty, were sent out from the protection of their villages to suffer terrible privation in their search for a "spirit" that would reveal itself to them. If the young man was sincere and his vision true, his benefactor, be it a black fish, a wolf, an eagle, or any other creature, would keep him from harm and give him special powers for his entire adult life.

11

The young seeker could receive the cunning of the raven, the power of the eagle, the hunting skill of the wolf, or the swimming ability of the black fish. Again, perhaps it would be the spirit of the salmon, making him a great fisherman, or it could be a gift from the cedar tree, bringing him the skill to carve.

His gift would bring him honor and wealth provided he did nothing to discredit the "spirit power." Any form of dishonesty or deceit would precipitate an abrupt end to the arrangement, and the unfortunate man would suffer disgrace, perhaps even exile from the village.

Much of the "spirit power," which was painfully sought and proudly possessed, was concerned with the procurement of food. The hunter and the fisherman each possessed his own special gift that brought him a bountiful food supply by magical means. One story of such a gift involves a club which was received as a supernatural power by a crippled boy. With it he was able to magically kill food animals. It enabled him to support himself and his old grandmother and to take his place in the tribal social structure. The club was passed on to another as a heritage and remains even today as a prominent part of the tribal culture.

An age-old story illustrates the use of "spirit power" for food procurement.

"In the quest for a spirit vision," another storyteller says, "it was necessary that the vision be a true one, honestly won through great suffering and privation. If a young man only pretended to have such a vision, sooner or later he would betray himself, with dire consequences.

"A certain young man had returned from his quest and an initiation ceremony and feast was being held for him. After the feasting and dancing, the time came for him to demonstrate the gift he had received.

"He rose before the assembled people and said, 'I want the young men of the village to go to the beach and pick up all the food that will be waiting for them there.'

"The people wondered at what he said, for they knew it was impossible to obtain food without hunting or fishing for it. The young men laughed in derision, but they agreed to go to the place that he named. There, to their surprise, they found fish of all kinds lying on the beach next to the high tideline. There were huge halibut, salmon, steelhead, cod, snapper, smelt, and herring. There were fish lying about that weren't even in season.

"The young men loaded all the fish into their canoes, which threatened to swamp with the great weight. Laboriously, they paddled back to the village. There was great excitement in the longhouse and everyone rejoiced, for now there would never be hunger in the village.

"This young man proved himself," the storyteller said. "Everyone knew that his gift was a true one. But in the crowd which was celebrating the initiation there was another young man. He was lazy and foolish. He had failed to carry out his quest for a vision and no one had much use for him.

"However, he was jealous of the boy who had succeeded, so he declared to everyone that he, too, had a gift and that it was just as good as the other young man's.

"So, an initiation ceremony was planned for him, too. And when the time came for him to show what his gift was, he instructed the young men of the village to go to a certain bay north of them, and there food would be waiting.

"But when the young men returned, their canoes were empty.

"'Where is the food I sent you for?' the boy asked.

"'There was none,' the young men replied in anger. 'We went where you told us to and we looked and looked. We stayed till it started to get dark. All we found was this one little spider crab.'

"The men dropped the crab at the initiate's feet. It was most unfortunate for him. The people have no use for a cheat. They made short work of this one." (They killed him.)

Many stories like this one were told to teach ethics to children. The central theme was often food and the customs concerning it. There were stories of the Salmonberry Bird who was such a glutton that he engaged in all sorts of trickery to get more than his share of the berries. There were stories of Raven, who tried to get others to hunt and carry his own game for him, and of Beaver and Mink, who refused to share their dinner.

The old songs reflected the need for magical powers in securing an abundance of food. With the beating drum as accompaniment, the singer would intone over and over again such phrases as:

come to me	*feed me*
come to me	*feed my family*
little brother	*feed my children*

Dances, too, reflected the importance of food gathering. In them one can often see the skilled hunter, one possessing great "spirit power," stalking his prey. Sometimes he is disguised as a deer, wearing a skin and shaking deer-hoof rattles as he gyrates and leaps about the area. Other times he may be an eagle, swooping and circling over his intended victim.

The origin of the Sxwaixwe mask, a dance mask unique to the Coast Salish, is food oriented. There are several versions of this story, as there are of the mask. One was told by an old man who claims direct descent from the first maker of the mask.

"Long ago," he said, "two children were playing on the beach. One was a girl about ten years old and the other was her brother who was younger. Soon the girl noticed that a salmon was swimming in the shallow water near them. It seemed to be trying to attract their attention.

"The children ran out into the water and the fish called to them. 'I have a special gift for you,' he said. 'It is from the salmon people who live in the village under the sea nearby.'

"'What must we do?' asked the girl.

"'You must take me to your village. Put me in a cooking box and boil my flesh till it falls from my bones. Them throw my bones back into the shallow water where you found me. You will know what to do next.'

"The children did just as the salmon had instructed and when they had thrown the bones into the water, the bones separated and formed themselves into a mask unlike any that had ever been seen before.

"The boy and girl took the mask to their elders and told the story of how it came to be. To this day, the people carve replicas of that original Sxwaixwe mask."

Three versions of the Sxwaixwe mask

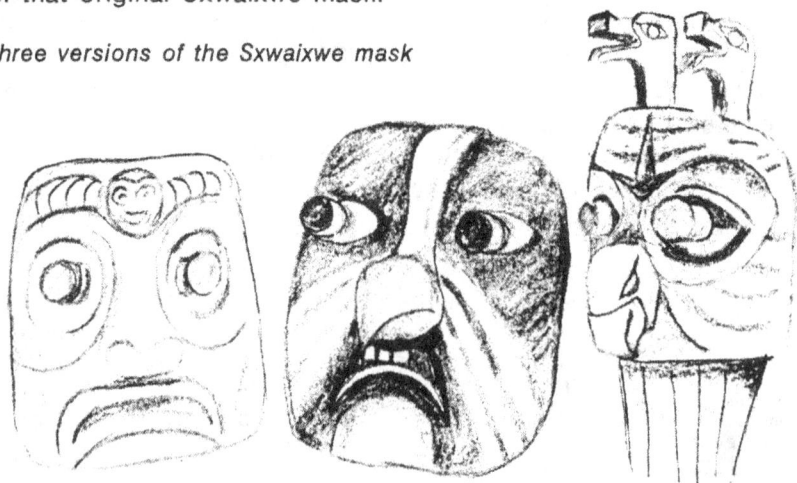

14

The Food Cycle 2

PAST THE FADING MEMORY of the oldest people, back into the depths of time, the Indian families have followed the route of Gha-hals each year, gathering the wealth that he laid out for them. The way was enriched with tradition, born of experience. The people knew when each food would be ready and waiting for them to gather. There was no deviating; ceremonies were observed, and if all was done properly, there was ample food for all until the next food cycle.

March — When the herring arrived in the bays and estuaries to spawn in March, the people put aside their winter occupations. It was time to begin the business of gathering herring spawn to add fresh food to their larders.

They had devised a clever way of assuring themselves an ample supply of this delicacy with a minimum of labor. Cut cedar branches were intertwined to form a dense, matted surface. These were laid along the shore where the herring habitually came to spawn. The fish found these devices especially to their liking, and they would deposit their egg masses along the branches. Later, the people gathered the branches and laid them on racks over slow-smoking fires to cure the eggs. Such delicately seasoned roe provided a gourmet treat that could rival the finest Russian caviar.

April — By April, when the ducks were passing overhead on their northern migration, the hunter was ready. The ducks settled into the bays and estuaries to feed and rest, and the people found it simple and efficient to erect nets along the shore. These nets, tightly woven of nettle twine, were tied between trees or tall poles along the same area where the cedar branches had been placed to entice the herring to deposit roe. While the hunter was busily gathering the branches, he would startle the feeding ducks. They would fly into the nets and become entangled.

Usually the ducks were barbecued on the spot, using either a spit or a rack over a trench fire. For people who had been subsisting on dried food for several months, barbecued duck was a welcome change. It marked the beginning of the fresh food cycle.

May — With the coming of the warm days of May, the people began preparations for their annual food-gathering odyssey, which would take them to a number of islands, back to the mainland beaches, up the rivers, and into the mountains.

Moving an entire village, with children, dogs, and equipment, required extensive preparations. Split cedar boards were removed from the walls of the village houses and lashed across wide freight canoes to form sturdy rafts. Mats, poles, baskets, utensils, clothing, and hunting and fishing equipment were all carefully stowed aboard.

The first stops were islands where the camas beds were ready to harvest. Each woman had a small area that was hers to dig, and eventually pass on to a member of her family when she could no longer endure the backbreaking work.

The bulbs were dug very carefully, with sharp-pointed sticks that had been fire hardened. The method used was designed to conserve the beds, even to increase their yield over the years. Using her digger stick, the woman pried up the sod, bulbs and all. She extracted the large, mature bulbs from beneath the surface, leaving the bulblets intact to mature for another year. After this process, she carefully replaced the sod and moved on to another section.

When the camas had been dug, the work of processing it for winter storage began, but not until the group held a feast. This onion-like member of the lily family was a favorite vegetable, highly prized, even craved by the Indian diner. To bring out its best qualities, it was baked in a pit for a long time: until it was mellow and creamy in texture. Everyone gorged until they could hold no more, a camas orgy. Then at last, their craving appeased, the serious work of baking, drying, pounding, and storing this important staple began.

While the women were laboring, the men and boys trolled for spring salmon. Just as the women had special locations in the camas fields which were theirs by inheritance, the men owned fishing territories. Fishing gear that had been prepared during the leisure hours of winter now came into use. There were hooks finely made from knots of the hemlock tree, tough twine created from twisted inner cedar bark, and fish clubs carved from maple.

June — By June, salmon trolling was begun in earnest. The first spring salmon caught was occasion for one of the most meaningful ceremonies practiced by the people. In order to assure an abundant run of salmon, so necessary to the survival of the Indians, the first salmon caught was treated as an honored guest.

When the fisherman brought it to shore, he called to his children to prepare a bed of ferns. This was the signal for the entire summer encampment to assemble for the salmon ceremony, in which the children played an important part.

When the ferns had been prepared, the salmon was carefully laid on them and the children carried it to the camp, singing the "Salmon Song." Here everyone gathered. They welcomed their guest with the "Welcome Song."

Then the *siem* or head man of the village greeted it and told the salmon: "You are an honored guest. We welcome you to our village and hope that you will consider that we are your friends. We will give you a new life now. We will place your bones in the water. Then you will be able to swim back to your salmon village under the sea and tell all your people how kind we have been to you. Bring many of them back with you. We will honor them too."

The salmon was cleaned and roasted whole. When it was done to perfection, it was given to the children to eat. This was the only time that children were allowed to eat first, or to take part in a ceremony.

If the salmon was pleased, it would tell all the salmon people about the fine treatment it received. The people could then expect a great salmon run as all the salmon people came to visit.

July — In July, the group moved on to other islands to set up their summer camps. It was time for the men to set out reef nets to gather in the hoards of salmon that would soon begin to migrate past the fishing locations.

Reef-netting gear configuration

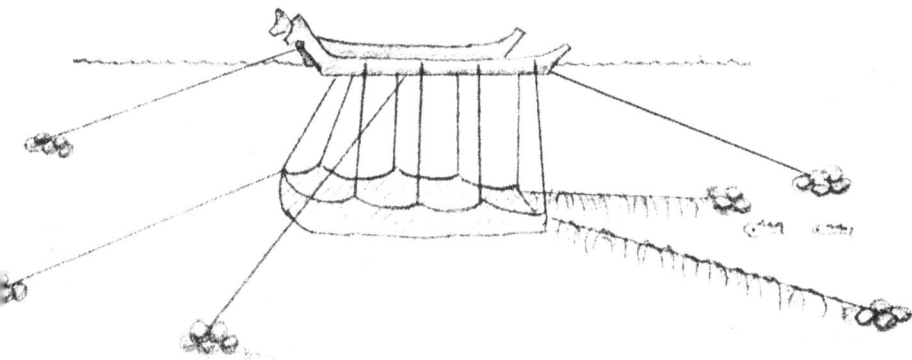

17

The whole encampment gathered willow branches to make the nets for this unique type of fishing. Once the long nets had been constructed, they were strung between a pair of anchored canoes. Lines disguised by seaweed were laid to guide the salmon into the net, which was quickly raised to snare fish. The bulk of the people's salmon was caught by using this reef-netting technique.

The salmon were prepared for winter storage by the women. Huge drying fires and racks were set up on the beaches adjacent to the reef-netting operation. While the men fished, the women spent their days cleaning and drying. The supply of fish seemed to be endless.

When the catch finally dwindled, the women and girls turned their attention to berrying. This they enjoyed. At last they could turn their backs on the endless work of fish processing and leave the camps for hours at a time. They picked into baskets suspended from their heads by tumplines. This left their hands free to pick. Some of the berries were eaten fresh. The surplus was dried in the sun and pounded into cakes for winter use.

Fern roots were gathered, too, to be roasted and eaten at camp, or to be dried and powdered for use as a flour during the cold, wet winter days.

August — Sometime in August the women would roll up the mats and gather together their utensils and equipment in preparation for the next move. The flotilla then moved to other islands with good clam beds. It was time to begin the backbreaking task of clam digging. This task fell to the women also. The men engaged in the chase, hunting the small island deer and netting ducks, now beginning to migrate south.

September — In September, the air was filled with smoke from the drying fires. Row upon row of clams hung above the smoking wood. Horse clams, butter clams, and littlenecks were packed in baskets and storage boxes for winter use. The task of digging and processing was a challenge to the strength and tenacity of the women, but it was vitally important. Next to the salmon, clams ranked as the basic staple in the people's diet.

Woven cedar-bark nets, stretched across narrow island isthmuses, yielded hunters an ample supply of fresh venison. It was baked in a pit or barbecued on spits. Surplus meat was cut in strips and sun-dried for a winter treat.

October — With the coming of cool weather, the people gathered together their accumulated food supplies and began their homeward expedition. It was a roundabout trip, for they had cached supplies at each gathering location. Now it must all be garnered into the canoes and carried to permanent winter villages.

When at last, after months of work and adventure in their island domain, the people returned to their permanent homes, there was still much to be done. The rafts were dismantled and the boards replaced on the walls of the great houses. The food was carefully packed into containers that had been specially prepared: airtight wooden boxes for some, porous baskets for other kinds of supplies.

Then the families traveled up the coastal rivers in search of blueberries, bear, deer, and mountain goat. This was an awesome thing for them, for they feared the dark, somber forests and the towering mountains which were so different from the beaches and open water that they knew so well. These trips were made as quickly as possible, and with all the "spirit power" protection that they could evoke.

November — By November, the storage boxes were full and a safe, comfortable winter was assured. There was always that little bit more to do: that last fish to catch, late-migrating brant to snare, or seals to hunt. The fishermen spent the dark, rainy days of November bringing in the surplus that could mean the difference between plenty and affluence. Already the women had moved into the longhouses. Mats were hung along the walls, separating the family groups. Food was stored on the shelves overhead. Cooking fires were built on the dirt floor, one beneath each smoke hole.

December — A sense of muted excitement filled the December air. The time of the potlatches and winter ceremonials was approaching. Carvers repaired ceremonial equipment, which included masks, rattles, and drums. Women created beautiful baskets, using the reeds and roots they had gathered during the summer trek.

The gathering had been completed. Until the next warm days of spring, the energies of the people would be spent in show of their wealth and "spirit power." Now was the time when great families would become greater, or be humbled, depending on the success of their yearly gathering expedition, the prowess of their hunters and fishers, and the skill and stamina of their women. It was also the time when the young and the ambitious could pit themselves against the established leadership in a struggle to attain recognition and prestige, according to their achievements.

As the winter winds blew colder, the rains came in unceasing monotony, the people gathered around the fires in their longhouses. This was the time when the cultural traditions of the tribe were most apparent. Old men, revered for their wisdom and knowledge of the ancient days, recounted myths and tales of greatness. Children, particularly, were expected to sit for hours while the storyteller told long, involved sagas of legendary creatures and heroes.

January — The time of potlatches had come! All the work of the previous year now would become important. The food that had been gathered and stored would provide the basis for great feasts of such abundance that precious fish oil would be tossed upon the blazing fires in the longhouses with such abandon that rafters were singed. Baskets and blankets, laboriously made around the winter fires, were displayed as a symbol of family wealth. All this show of riches was used to impress other villages with the great power possessed by the family; power expressed by plenty of food, worldly goods, "spirit power," and prestige.

February — The winter ceremonies had come to an end. It was time, once again, to think of the quest for food. Canoes were carved or repaired. Fishing gear was made. Arrow and spear points were flaked. The preparation for another year of adventure among the bays, estuaries, islands, and rivers began again.

Cooking Equipment 3

THE COAST SALISH INDIANS used three basic methods of food preparation: pit cookery, spit or rack cookery, and simmering. All were simple, required a minimum of equipment, and would be as useful today for campers and picnickers as they were for daily living over a hundred years ago.

Since the villages were located on or near beaches, this type of environment figures in the cookery. If you try some of the recipes given later and wish to work in an authentic fashion, it is necessary that you work on a gently sloping gravel beach, or in an area with loose soil and a supply of rocks, seaweed, ferns, and hardwood.

While some cooking equipment was expendable, used once and discarded, much of it was beautifully made and was highly prized by the women who owned it. Baskets woven of split cedar roots and decorated with the skin of wild cherry and birch bark were so tight that they held water. Ladles and spoons were carved from maple. Cooking boxes of cedar were made from a single, steamed and bent board. Tongs were fashioned from a split, hardwood shoot.

Cooking equipment: wooden tray, bent-wood box, tongs and serving ladle, cooking basket, rocks, and cattail mat

21

Spits (skewers for meat) were carved from ocean spray, called iron wood by the Indians (a spirea shrub of the rose family). Directions for making these accessories will be given at appropriate places. This is done more for information than as a suggestion that these articles be fashioned since materials are difficult to obtain and the skill required is the result of much patience and practice.

Imu pit with wooden digging stick, rocks, seaweed, and tongs

Equipment for pit cookery — Pit cookery was a type of imu and involved baking or steaming in a pit, depending on the method used. Wet seaweed created a steam environment, while the use of leaves or ferns resulted in a baked product. Many types of food, ranging from a shore dinner to roast duck, were prepared in this manner.

Materials used for pit cookery were few and easy to find. An implement to dig a pit about two feet deep and long enough and wide enough to accommodate the food to be prepared was necessary. Today, we would simply use a shovel, but the Indians used a wide stick.

Stones that could be heated until they glowed without splitting or exploding were needed. Women chose rocks that were of volcanic origin, such as basalt or dense lava rocks that had been worn to a round shape. Open or porous rocks such as granite or schist ex-

22

ploded under the great heat of the imu, while sedimentary types, such as slate or shale, burst open along seams. If in doubt, choose rocks that are heavy for their size and of smooth texture.

Ferns, leaves, or seaweed for food wrapping were needed. The taste and texture required often indicated the appropriate wrapping. The various kinds of wrapping materials were all easily found on northwest beaches.

Ribbon seaweed was preferred, and it could be found heaped in mounds along the high tidelines of bays and inlets of Puget Sound. Iron wood leaves were prized by the Indians for the delightful flavor they imparted to the food, and were used particularly with game. Ferns also were very satisfactory. A variety were used, the best being bracken, sword, and maiden (lady) ferns.

Tongs were needed to lift hot rocks. Preferably, they were fashioned from the slender, upright shoots of iron wood. This wood was particularly prized by Indian cooks because it was highly heat resistant. When fire hardened it was almost impervious to heat and flame. Other woods, such as green maple, birch, or alder, were used if iron wood was not available.

Making tongs: To make tongs, select a branch or shoot of iron wood that is straight, true, and about 1" thick. If iron wood is not available, other woods such as alder, maple, or birch will do. Cut off a stick 15" to 18" in length. Split it up the center for about two-thirds the length. Insert a small wedge at the split to hold the tongs open about 2". Wrap the stick tightly at the end of the split to keep it from splitting farther. Salish women used split cedar bark for the purpose, but twine will work and is much easier for us to acquire today.

To use, force the tongs down on a rock until the rock is wedged securely. Pick the rock up and tap the tongs lightly on the pot to loosen the rock, allowing it to fall into the water. Rocks are removed from the pot in the same way.

Equipment for spit cookery — Spit cookery involved the placement of meat pieces on spits or skewers that were angled over a fire for barbecuing. The spits were made from iron wood. No other wood would do, since only iron wood would endure the intense heat of alder coals. Fortunately, iron wood grew abundantly near the bays and beaches of Puget Sound. It still does.

Spits were pushed into the ground at an angle over the fire or were laid at an angle against a single bar rack.

Making spits and a single bar rack: Barbecuing spits are highly prized by Indian barbecuers today, as they were hundreds of years ago. Making good spits is an art. Much time and effort is involved in creating these implements, but the results are worth the effort. Some spits still in use today are over fifty years old. With care, they will last another fifty.

Cut iron wood in the spring when the sap first goes up. At this time the bark peels off easily. Peel the limbs and trim them to about 3' long. Split them lengthwise. Two flat spits can be made from each length of wood.

Use a sharp knife to taper the ends to a point, beginning about 5" from each end. It is necessary that the spits be satin smooth, so that food can be slipped on and off with a minimum of tearing. Sandpaper and a steel wool finish will accomplish this quite easily. Once the wood is smooth, treat the entire spit with salad oil, allowing it to soak in to create a permanent surface. Cure until it is completely dry and nonsticky.

The final step is the hardening process. Heat the spit near a slow fire and gradually move the spit closer to the fire until it becomes dense and virtually fire resistant.

In the old days, the spits were made in the same manner, but with different tools and materials. The iron wood was split with bone, shell, or stone tools. A piece of dogfish skin, which is as abrasive as sandpaper, was used to smooth the spit. Fish oil or seal fat was used to finish and season the spit.

Spits are usually pushed directly into the ground at the fire's edge and angled over the fire so that meat or fish will cook readily. At times a rack is positioned in such a way that the tips of the spits will rest against it. This device is useful when the ground or beach cannot support the weight of the skewered spits.

To make the single bar rack, select hardwood saplings 1" in diameter. Cut 4 poles 4' long and sharpen the larger ends. At one side of the fire pound 2 of the sharpened poles into the ground so that they are about 2' apart and angled so their tips cross within 6" of the top ends.

Place the other pair of poles in a similar configuration at the other side of the fire. Lay a fifth hardwood pole within the "V" where the pole pairs cross to form the horizontal bar. Adjusting the angles of the crossing pole pairs will place the "Vs" higher or lower above the fire. This adjustment will regulate the height of the horizontal crossbar to the flames.

Fish on spits leaning against a single pole rack

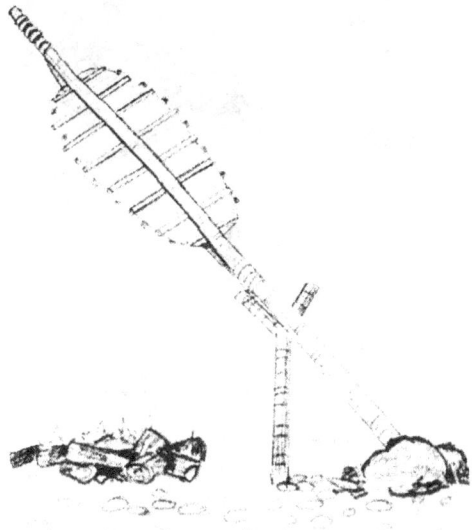

Split-pole barbecue rack

Equipment for rack cookery — Rack cookery, of which there were several versions, was another method for barbecuing shellfish, fish, and game.

SPLIT-POLE METHOD: A very ingenious method for barbecuing a single fish was devised by Salish women. The fish was encased within a split-pole rack that provided proper placement above the fire. The equipment needed was usually made on the spot, for one-time use. It would be just as convenient and easy to make today. In fact, with our considerable advantage in tools, we would have a better time of it.

Making a split-pole rack: The ideal material for making the rack is a maple sapling about 2" in diameter and 5' long. Maple is a hardwood, relatively heat resistant, and is quite prolific on the northwest coast. However, if no maple is to be found in the area, you can use alder or birch as quite acceptable substitutes.

Fashion crosspieces of green cedar about 18" long. They should be split into sticks about ½" X 1". As an alternative, use small trimmed and peeled branches. Since cedar burns readily, it must be green—even soaked in water—before being used as barbecue equipment.

To make the rack, split the sapling down the middle, beginning at the smaller end. Make the split slightly longer than the size of

Barbecue rack

the fish to be cooked. Fry the split ends apart and prop them open. Lay half of the cedar sticks on one side of the split. Carefully lay the opened fish on the sticks. Then lay the rest of the sticks on top of the fish.

Release the sapling from the prop, so that it closes upon the cross-sticks and pinches the fish. Exert pressure and wire or tie the ends of the pole together. The Indians used twine made of cedar bark or nettle fiber to tie the pole ends. Today, a piece of wire or heavy twine will make a good substitute.

The fish is now ready to barbecue according to recipes given in the recipe section.

LARGE RACK METHOD: This highly useful method of cookery was employed when a large amount of food was to be cooked. Anything from venison to ducks to fish and crabs could be easily and deliciously prepared on a rack erected over glowing coals. The rack was made on the spot from iron wood or green hardwood saplings. The beauty of it was that a whole banquet could be cooked on the same rack with no danger that one food would flavor the other, as was the case with the imu.

Making a barbecue rack: Cut 10 sturdy hardwood poles about 5' long (iron wood is best), and 20 smaller sticks about 3' long. Place a pair of the longer poles at each of the 4 corners, a reasonable distance from the fire (making a rectangle about 4½' x 2½'). Angle the pairs in such a way that their bases are 2' apart and their tops cross. Pound them well into the ground. Lay the remaining 2 poles between each of 2 pairs of posts to form a horizontal framework. Place the smaller sticks across these crosspieces to form a grid about 4' off the ground on which to place the food to be barbecued.

26

Equipment for simmering food (basket and box cooking) —
Basket cooking was done in the winter, when families were forced
to rely on the dried, preserved food they had gathered earlier. Warm-
ing fires glowed day and night down the center of the longhouses,
so cooking facilities for simmering were readily available.

Red-hot rocks were dropped into water-filled, watertight baskets and boxes. Food was added as the water began to boil. As
the rocks cooled, they were removed with heat-resistant, iron wood
tongs and replaced with more hot stones. Water in the basket was
kept at the boiling point until food was cooked into a stew or soup.

Baskets destined to become cooking pots were made of the
finest materials available, the strong, straight fibers found in roots
of the giant red cedar which grew so prolifically along the coast.
The roots were pulled from the soil in the spring. They were cleaned,
skinned, and coiled to dry until winter, when there was leisure time
that could be devoted to basketry.

To make a coiled basket, the women needed patience to the
point of exhaustion. There was much to be learned and the learning
could only come by doing. No one can tell another how the split
cedar should feel when it has soaked just long enough to be right
for "sewing" the basket together. No one can tell another just how
tight to pull the stitches. These things had to be felt.

Indian simmering techniques are nearly impossible to
reproduce today. Any cooking baskets still in existence would be
far too valuable to risk cooking in, and they are much too tedious
to make, even if raw materials can be found. The few remaining cooking boxes, formed from a single plank of cedar, are museum pieces.
Those who wish to try Indian simmering techniques will have to use
a heavy iron pot or a large fireproof bowl or casserole as a substitute.

Cooking Fires

4

INDIANS devised a number of types of fires designed to accommodate various methods of cookery. They were all kept to a minimum size. There is far more heat in a bed of glowing alder coals than in a crackling fire of cedar; it also lasts much longer.

Dry cedar twigs, sometimes called "squaw wood," are best for starting fires. Such kindling is available wherever there are large cedar trees. It will ignite quickly, without the use of paper, and burn in a rainstorm. Look for dead lower branches which grow near the ground. The tip ends are brittle and will crumble easily in your hands. Wad several handfuls together and place them in a scooped-out hollow in the sand, gravel, or dirt. Break the rest of the branches into short lengths and place tepee fashion around the tinder.

Check for the wind and place igneous-type rocks around the firepit, taking care to protect the fire from strong breezes. The Indian used a fire drill to produce a spark to light his fire. No one but the most dedicated purist would attempt this today. A match is quite acceptable. Lay on hardwood, log cabin fashion, when the tepee is burning briskly. Allow it to burn down to a bed of coals. After this, add wood sparingly, to keep and perpetuate the glowing heat.

The type of firewood used determines the degree of heat, the length of cooking time, and to a certain extent the texture and flavor of the food produced. The Indians preferred alder, considering it to be the best all-around wood. It ignites readily, gives a good steady

split cedar

cedar kindling

squaw wood

paper

alder

Tepee fire

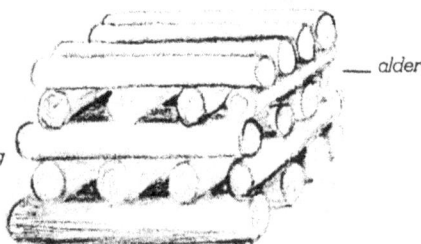

Build a log cabin fire over the tepee fire for a quick hot bed of coals

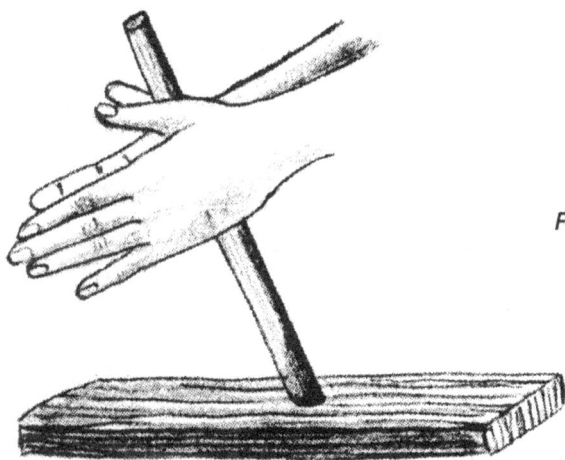

Fire drill

heat, burns slowly, and forms glowing coals. As a bonus, it imparts a delicious, smoky flavor to the food cooked over it. Cherry is a harder wood than alder and will burn longer, but it is more difficult to ignite and may smolder rather than form and hold coals. Maple will burn for a long time, but it is harder to find and cut. Birch is fast burning and not as hot as the other woods. Even so, if alder is not available, these other woods will do nicely.

Cedar was never used since it flares, sending out sparks, burns too quickly, and does not make good coals. Cedar bark, on the other hand, will burn to excellent hot coals if added to other woods when the fire is burning nicely. Fir is not desired either, for it burns too quickly and is full of pitch that will sputter and flare.

The Coast Salish made fire with a simple fire drill, but found that it was much easier to keep a fire alive than to start one. In the longhouses, coals at the hearths were kept glowing throughout the night. Kindling was added and the coals were fanned into flames the next morning. While traveling, the people carried coals or punks of braided cedar or fern root in clamshells.

Types of Fires

Pit fire or Imu — Used for steaming or roasting, this type of fire was built in a pit or trench dug out of beach gravel well above the high tideline. Depending on the type and volume of food to be cooked, the size of the excavation will vary from one about 2' deep, 3' wide, and 6' long to a mini-pit 1' deep and 2' square. Whatever the size, the procedure is the same.

After the pit or trench is dug, lay large igneous-type stones, about 3" to 6" diameter, in the trench. Start a fire in the trench on top of the rocks, using the standard procedure with cedar tinder and kindling. When the fire is burning nicely, add alder. As the fire burns down and glowing coals form, spread the coals on the rocks. Add wood to build more coals.

After several hours, the entire pit will be filled with a bed of glowing coals and the heat will be intense. At this point, have the food ready for the imu, so that it can be very quickly placed in the pit at the proper time.

Using a rake, remove the coals to the side of the pit. Rake some of the hot stones aside as well. Place the food on top of the rocks according to the directions of the recipe you are following. When the food is covered and ready, place some of the hot rocks on top of it. Using the rake, cover the whole contents quickly with beach gravel. Be sure to mark the area well so that some unwary beach walker or playing child does not run across the hot gravel.

Hot rocks fire — Much Indian cookery was done by the boiling water method, particularly in the winter when dried food was utilized. Rocks were heated in the coals of a fire and added to water in baskets or cedar boxes. The rocks brought the water to the boiling point.

It was a popular way to cook, for every kitchen midden yields an ample supply of these round volcanic rocks, once prized possessions of an Indian cook.

The fire devised to heat these rocks is small and simple. Begin with cedar kindling. Add small pieces of alder or any other hardwood. The aim is to create a source of intense heat, which comes only from glowing coals.

Place the rocks close to the fire on top of other rocks, usually large and flat, to keep them as free of ashes as possible. Place a log, boulder, or other reflector on the other side of the rocks to increase the heat. Rocks must be constantly rotated, moved about to heat evenly, popped into the cooking basket, and removed and returned to the fire for reheating when they are cool. The Indians quickly rinsed the rocks in a second basket of water before they were dropped into the food. This cleaned the rocks of ash without greatly reducing their heat.

With our modern age, when even a tin can makes an acceptable pot, cooking with rocks may seem to be inconvenient. For those who do not want to experiment with this age-old method, by all means use a kettle over a fire. You can still make an Indian-style stew and it will taste just like the one made with hot rocks.

The fire for this pot cookery is still kept small. Once it is going, cedar bark or any small pieces of beach wood will do to produce the necessary coals.

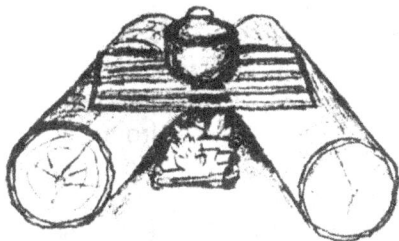

Hunter-trapper fire — This type of fire is ideal for cooking on. Angle two small logs, about 9" to 12" in diameter, so that the ends meet. Build the fire in this angle. Place the pot on a rack laid across the logs or on a rock set in the angle. As the logs burn, shove them together to give more shelter to the fire.

Caution: be sure the fire is thoroughly out before leaving, as fire can work its way into a log and smolder for some time before bursting into flame.

Hot rocks fire   Hunter-trapper fire

Barbecue fire — The same basic fire was used for barbecuing whether it was done for a feast for hundreds or for a family dinner. Clear a space around the fire area for a distance of 4'. Dig a trench or pit 1' deep and of the size and shape required for the type of barbecue used. Start the fire in the pit by using cedar twigs or split kindling. Add larger cedar sticks till the fire is crackling merrily. Then add small sticks of alder, maple, cherry, or other hardwood. When the small wood is burning well, gradually add bigger pieces. The aim here is to build a 2" to 5" bed of glowing coals that will give off a steady, intense heat for an hour or more. When the fire has produced sufficient coals, allow it to die down; add more wood only if it becomes necessary to maintain the level of heat.

The large rack barbecue requires a firepit that is several feet smaller than the size of the rack to be used so that the fire will cook the food but not burn the rack supports. Generally a firepit that is 2' X 3' will be adequate for a rack that is 3' X 5'.

31

For a spit barbecue, the fire is built in a trench that is long enough to accommodate the volume of food to be prepared. Some tribal celebrations feature barbecued salmon cooked by the ton on spits ranged along pits up to 50' long. To get the maximum reflected heat from the coals, the trench should be no more than 2' wide by 1' deep. If it is more convenient, cement blocks or volcanic stone walls may be built along the fire to a height of 1' or more to reflect the heat. Build the fire by starting many small fires the length of the trench. As they enlarge, they will form one continuous blaze.

Smoking fire — This type of fire was used for smoking fish, clams, and meats. It produces lots of smoke but no heat, since the goal was to preserve the food by curing it, not cooking it.

Start the fire in the usual manner. Use an enclosed area to confine the smoke as much as possible. Keep smoking fires very small. Add very green wood once the fire is going well and some coals have formed. Soft wood such as fir or hemlock may be used, provided it is very wet and green. However, other woods such as hickory, alder, maple, cherry, or even apple are more acceptable since they add an aroma of their own to the finished product.

The wood should smolder rather than burn. Add it sparingly a piece at a time to keep the smoke coming. Soft-smoked food is processed in several days using this method. Hard-smoked fish and meats take a week or more to thoroughly cure. Directions for smoking food is included in the recipe section.

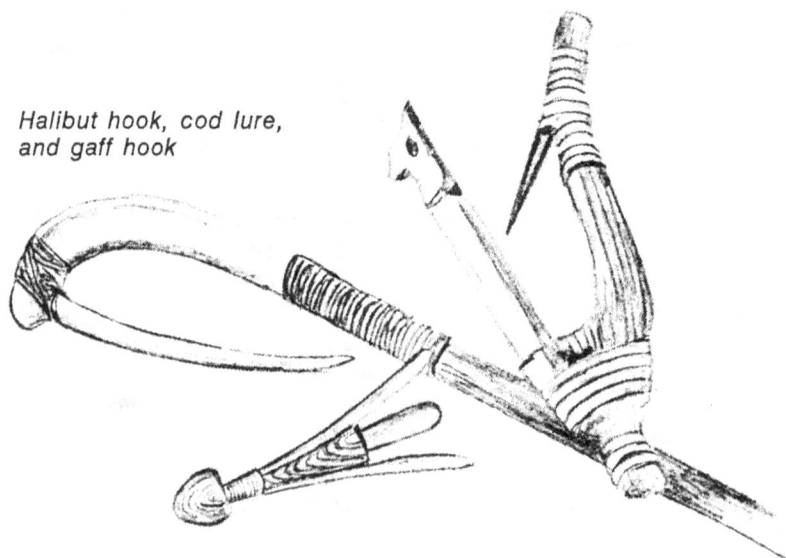

Halibut hook, cod lure, and gaff hook

Fish

 5

Salmon

A HUNDRED YEARS ago, the most important single item on the Coast Salish menu was salmon. It was an excellent fish; large, rich in oil, firm of flesh, delicate of flavor, and it lent itself equally well to various methods of preparation and preservation.

The runs of salmon were virtually unlimited in those days. "When the runs would come," the old-timers would say, "you could hear the swish-swish of their bodies through the water. The bays would turn silver and the rivers and spawning beds would be so glutted with fish you could walk across on their backs."

With this sort of bounty, it is easy to understand why a number of ways were devised to prepare the fish and why it dominated the Indian menu of long ago, as it does today. To prepare the fish, the people removed the backbone from the salmon. The method was to slit the flesh along the backbone after removal of the head and tail. The flensing knife was run along the backbone and ribs on both sides, cutting them away from the flesh. In this way, the opening was along the back of the fish, rather than along the abdomen as we are inclined to make it. When the fish was laid open along the back by the removal of the bone, the entrails were neatly exposed and were returned intact to the sea.

Chum salmon

Male at bottom

Piece barbecue — Prepare a barbecue fire following directions on page 31. Cut the prepared fish into serving-sized pieces, about 3" square. Slip 4 pieces on each iron wood spit. Spits should be fashioned according to the directions on page 24. When all the salmon has been assembled in this way, and when the coals are right, place the spits in the ground or stand them against a rack at an angle that gives good exposure to the heat. The flesh side of the fish should be toward the fire. Watch the fish closely; the flesh should be seared and slightly browned.

When the aroma has become absolutely tantalizing and the pink color is now a rosy tan, turn the fish around so that the skin side is to the fire. Watch so that it does not burn. The salmon is rich in oil, which will cause the fire to sputter and flare, and it is possible that the fish itself can catch fire.

When the skin side has become crisp, turn again to the flesh side. Again, watch closely, for overdone fish is ruined fish. When it stops dripping, according to Indian cookery, it is done. If you wish to further test for doneness, flake a little with a fork. It should be moist and flake easily, but it should not be crumbly or dry.

Remove the fish from the fire immediately. Service may be direct from the spit, or from a platter. Serve at once. Arrange to wrap any second helpings to retain the heat.

Whole fish barbecue (split-pole rack) — This method is ideal for preparing one medium-sized fish, enough to serve 4 to 8 people.

Build a barbecue fire according to directions on page 31. While the fire is burning down to coals, make a split-pole rack according to directions on page 25. Clean and debone the fish according to page 33. Season as desired.

Lay the fish on the split-pole rack. Secure by twisting with a piece of wire. A little pressure will have to be used to keep the whole apparatus firm throughout the cooking process.

When the coals are ready, place the split-pole rack at an angle about 2½' above the heat. The split-pole rack may be laid against a post and crosspiece structure, propped against a log, or set in a crotch support.

Place the split-pole rack so that the flesh side of the fish is over the coals. Seal in the juices by toasting the fish to a golden brown. Watch closely because the fish oil will cause the fire to flare.

When the flesh is crispy to the touch, turn the fish skin side to the fire. Allow that to crisp also. Watch the dripping oil. Turn the fish again when the dripping has almost stopped. Reheat the flesh side and remove from the fire when the fish no longer drips oil. Remove the split-pole rack. Take off the top layer of supports, but use the bottom sticks as a serving platter. Serve immediately—the hotter the better.

Standard rack barbecue — The standard rack barbecue is the most commonly known barbecue process today. The white man has borrowed it from the Indian and innovated it to the point that the Sunday backyard event usually bears little resemblance to the original concept.

Because the wooden barbecue rack was placed directly over the fire, the use of rack cookery was limited to quickly cooked food and smoked delicacies where there was little direct heat. For this reason, if you are following authentic Indian methods, only small filleted salmon should be used so that the actual cooking time is about half an hour. However, you need not limit your fare to salmon. Oysters on the half shell, steamer clams, and other quickly cooked food can be laid on the rack alongside the fish. Recipes for these follow under appropriate headings.

To begin, build a barbecue fire according to direction on page 31. While the fire is burning to coals, make a rack according to directions on page 26.

Season the fish to your taste and lay it flesh side down on the rack. Allow it to sear to a golden brown to seal in the juices. Turn the fish skin side down and cook till it almost stops dripping. Return it to the original position for a few minutes. Watch it closely; when done, the flesh must still be moist and easily flaked into sections. Serve immediately.

Baking salmon — A large, whole salmon may be deliciously baked in a pit or imu. When this sort of cookery is done, it is customary to place a variety of food in the pit so that they all cook together, blending flavors and providing a bountiful, easily prepared meal. The method given for salmon is basic for all other food, which will be treated later under appropriate sections.

Build a pit fire according to directions on page 29. While the fire is burning to coals, gather the material you wish to use to wrap the fish. Indians preferred to wrap their salmon in the foliage of bracken ferns, which imparted a flavor that they relished. Other ferns or maple leaves will do, as will sand-free seaweed. Seaweed was gathered to lay under and over the wrapped fish as well, so you will need an ample supply. These materials are easily available on any saltwater beach. If you wish, foil may be substituted for ferns, and wet paper towels for the seaweed, but it is not really recommended, and would give you less than authentic Indian baked salmon.

Clean the salmon, but this time leave the backbone in. Lay a few slices of dry onion inside the fish and season according to your taste. In the old days, either dried or fresh camas were used to give a subtle, delicious flavor to the fish.

When the fire is ready, proceed with directions for preparing the imu on page 29. When all is prepared, place a layer of seaweed about 1" thick on the hot rocks. Lay the wrapped fish on this and cover it with an additional layer of seaweed. Place the extra hot rocks on top and cover all with gravel. Allow about 1 hour for a 10-pound salmon and add about 10 minutes per pound for each additional pound.

To remove your dinner from the imu, carefully scrape off the gravel and rocks and use two sticks to lift the salmon out of the pit, wrappings and all. Lay it on a plank or reasonably flat log and remove the top wrappings. Place another board or serving platter over the fish and invert. Remove the rest of the wrappings. Serve immediately, carefully cutting the flesh from the backbone as you serve. If you wish, the bone may be removed before serving by cutting along the back and peeling the flesh from the bone on both sides. However, this will take time and the fish will cool, losing some of its appeal.

Drying and smoking salmon for winter use — The Coast Salish method of preserving salmon is relished by gourmets; in fact we all become gourmets when this delicious food is served. Its proper preparation takes time and care, but the results are worth the additional effort. The Indians usually preferred chum salmon for smoking.

Allow a 2-day wait from the time the fish is caught to let it soften slightly and make preparations easier. Keep the fish well chilled. Rub it with dried sword ferns to remove the slime, or adopt today's materials and use crumpled newspaper. Use a sharp knife to remove the tail and head, including the gills. Make an incision down the backbone, then cut along the ribs on both sides. The backbone, with the entrails attached, can then be lifted out. The fish will open as a flat piece. If the salmon is large and has thick flesh, make 4 or more parallel lengthwise cuts in the flesh, almost through to the skin. This will let the smoke penetrate. Salmon over 20 pounds were often cut into strips for smoking.

Rub table salt well into the meat, to act as a curing agent, or soak the fish for up to 24 hours in a strong brine solution. If you use the brine method, rock salt is generally used, and the brine is right when a potato will float on top.

The fish must be properly spread and held above the fire for drying. Prepare a cedar "hanging" stick approximately 18" long and 1" in diameter. Round and smooth the stick lengthwise so that it can be easily inserted into the fish. Slide the hanging stick through slits made in the skin and flesh of the fish about 1/3 of the way down the fish from the head end. Cut several more cedar sticks approximately 1" wide and slightly shorter than the width of the salmon. Thin the ends to about 1/2 the width of the rest of the stick. Insert these sticks in the skin side of the salmon by placing the ends in cuts through the skin. This will spread the salmon wide. The spread salmon can now be hung over racks above the smoking fire. The top third of the fish will fall loosely over the hanging stick.

While the fire is being prepared, let the fish "rest." Stack fish atop each other, flesh to flesh. Proper stacking is important, since most Indian-caught fish were taken in rivers and it is impossible to remove all the slime from their skins.

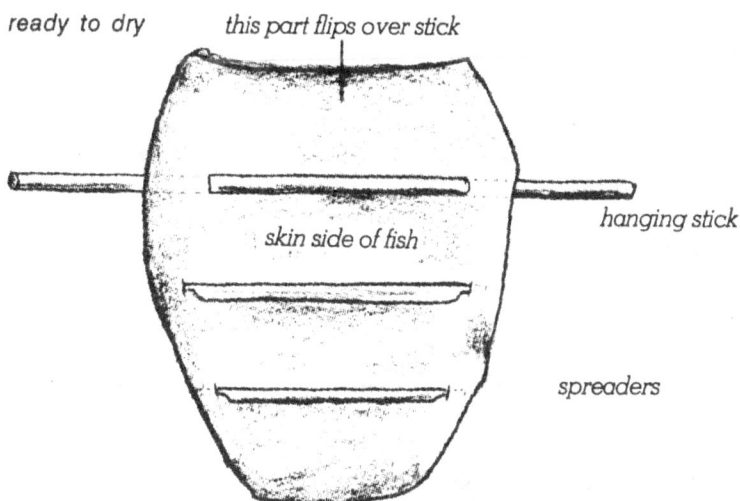

Salmon ready to dry   this part flips over stick

skin side of fish

hanging stick

spreaders

Alder wood is preferred for the fire, since it produces the best smoke and burns rather slowly. The object is to produce a volume of smoke with relatively little heat. There is a very fine line here, and the results will depend on how well you walk the wire. If your fire produces too much heat, the fish will cook and become leathery and tasteless. But enough heat is required to dry the fish. And, of course, there must be enough smoke to penetrate the fish and to aid in curing it as well as imparting the flavor typical of Indian smoked salmon.

Hang the fish above the fire when it is smoking freely and producing only a small amount of heat. Salmon is hung fairly high, 5' to 9' above the fire. In the old longhouses, smoking salmon often hung from the rafters above the cooking fire at a height of 15'.

The length of time required to smoke salmon depends on the type of finished product you desire. "Soft-smoked" fish require only two days of constant smoking. These fish will be rather soft and have a delicate smoky flavor. They will not keep. You must freeze or can them immediately and even then they should be well cooked before eating. "Hard-smoked," fully-dried fish, take a week or more to smoke. These fish will keep indefinitely. Leave them hanging until used. Hard-smoked salmon are of a leathery consistency and about ⅓ their original weight. Eat them as is, like beef jerky, if you have good teeth and are not afraid to exercise your jaws. The Indian way was to boil the fish for about 15 minutes. This restored the moisture and produced a tasty portion of fish for a dinner serving.

Salmon roe — Fish eggs were prized by Indians of the northwest, as a delicious food and as a valuable source of vitamins. Since herring and salmon were available in quantity, the roe of these fish was predominately used. However, eggs from any food fish may be processed by smoking and used in a variety of ways.

Of all fish, the salmon roe was the most valued. When the great salmon runs were under way, drying racks were erected on the beaches. The women worked countless hours cleaning the fish and hanging them over smoking fires to smoke and dry. The salmon roe was carefully removed, for it, too, was smoked and laid away for winter use.

During the great feasts and potlatches, thinly sliced strings of salmon eggs were served as appetizers, and were relished as caviar is today. The eggs were rich in nutritional value, and were also enjoyed as snacking food on long trips.

To prepare the roe for smoking, open the fish with care so that the egg sac does not split. The Indian method for splitting salmon, page 33, is ideal, for when the fish is laid open, the egg sac can simply be lifted out.

Split the sac and carefully remove the strings of eggs. Salt the roe and sprinkle it lightly with water and lemon juice to preserve the moisture. Lay the strings of eggs together, face to face. If possible, smoke them immediately, for the eggs will become increasingly "fishy" in flavor as they age. If immediate smoking is not possible, wrap the roe tightly in plastic film and refrigerate or freeze it until a convenient time for smoking.

To smoke the roe, prepare a smoke fire according to directions on page 32. Build a rack according to directions on page 26. You will need to modify the rack; a piece of screen laid over the rack is ideal. When the fire is smoking with little or no visible flame, lay the strings of eggs on the screen. Shield the fire as necessary to direct the smoke upward to the roe. Watch the fire, allowing smoke only. One or two pieces of green wood at a time should do the trick. A sprinkle of water now and then may help.

Salmon roe should smoke five or six hours at a minimum. When done, it will be firm, considerably reduced in size, and dark brown in color. It will smell decidedly smoky. The Indian women stored their supply of cured roe in airtight baskets on shelves above their family compartments in the winter longhouse. Today, wrap it tightly and refrigerate. To serve, slice the smoked roe very thin.

Cod and other bottom fish

A variety of cod and other bottom fish were caught and relished by the Coast Salish Indians. Cod, sole, perch, snapper, and an assortment of rockfish lurked about the reefs that lie off Puget Sound beaches. None were as plentiful as the salmon, nor as highly prized, but they added variety to the menu and could be caught throughout the year, assuring fresh fish between the great salmon runs.

Because of its delicate flesh, cod required care when barbecued on spits, but they were easily handled when cooked on a rack or in an imu pit. Ling cod was much preferred over black, not only for its relatively large size, but also for its delicate flavor and firmer texture.

For barbecuing cod, build a fire as described on page 31. Allow the fire to die to glowing coals. Prepare the fish by removing the head and tail. Clean it as described on page 33. The head and tail may be reserved for soup if desired (see chowder recipe, page 47).

Spit barbecue — Cut a large cod into 4" or 5" square pieces. Insert the spits into the meat and angle the spits over the fire as indicated on page 23.

Sear the flesh side till it turns a golden brown and the flesh is slightly crusted. Then turn the skin side toward the fire and cook this side until it stops dripping. Special care must be taken to assure that the fish does not fall from the spit while cooking. Remember that fish cooks quickly. It is done when it flakes easily clear to the skin.

Split-pole barbecue — Any size of cod or bottom fish may be barbecued using the split-pole method as explained on page 25. When the fire has died to coals, angle the rack over the fire to sear the flesh side. When it is golden brown and crusted over, turn the skin side to the fire. Cook it until the juices stop dripping and the flesh flakes easily to the skin.

Large rack barbecue — A number of small cod, snapper, or rockfish may be cooked using this rack method, which also lends itself to a complete shore dinner — simply add oysters, clams, crabs, and vegetables. All food must be of the type that cooks quickly, in 20 minutes or less, for prolonged cooking is liable to burn the rack before the food is done.

Build the fire following directions on page 31. While the fire is burning to coals, build the rack according to page 26.

The fish may be filleted or in this case, since the fish are small, cleaned in the conventional manner and cooked whole. Season if you wish, or enjoy the pure, smoked flavor.

Place the fish on the rack, along with whatever else you plan to cook. Carefully turn to cook both sides. A deviation from Indian tongs or sticks is recommended. Use a wide spatula or turner.

If the fish is quite small, another non-Indian innovation is suggested. Lay a sheet of foil over the crosspieces of the rack, puncture it liberally to let the smoke through, and place the fish on it for cooking.

Watch carefully, for the fish will be done almost as soon as it has been laid on the rack. If you use foil, remove it with the fish intact and serve the fish immediately.

Cod fish bake — A large black or ling cod lends itself to the Indian imu method. Like the salmon, it may be baked alone or with other seafood and vegetables for a complete single-effort meal.

Clean the fish by slitting it from the anus to the abdomen. Remove the entrails. The Indians saved the roe and disposed of the rest by returning it to the sea.

The method of cooking is the same as for baked salmon, with a few differences. The head may be baked with the fish—the cheeks and eyes were considered delicacies—or it may be severed and used for a soup or stew.

Prepare the fire according to page 29. While the fire is burning to coals, gather materials for wrapping the fish. Use wet seaweed for the outer wrap and leaves for the inner covering. The leaves of the iron wood bush are desired, for they impart a delightful flavor to the bland flesh of the cod. Ferns or maple leaves will do, however.

Brush the top coals from the fire along with some of the rocks. Lay the seaweed on the remaining coals and rocks, put the wrapped fish on it, and lay more seaweed on top. Return the coals and hot rocks to cover the fish and heap gravel over all. Mark the spot.

Cod fish has a softer texture than salmon and will cook faster. A 5-pound cod should cook to perfection in ½ hour. Allow about 8 minutes a pound for each additional pound.

Open the pit at one end, expose the fish and test it for doneness with a stick. The flesh should be white and flaky and the skin should peel off easily. Take care not to overcook.

Halibut

The firm, sweet, white flesh of the halibut was highly prized among Coast Salish people. One of these fish, often as big as a bathtub, provided a feast for an entire village. Whatever was left over was cut into strips and hung above a smoky fire to cure for winter use.

To prepare the fish, remove the backbone, cut along the side from head to tail, and carefully pare the flesh from the bones. Remove the head and tail and lay the fish out flat. Remove and discard the entrails. You may wish to save the cheeks; they are choice. The head makes a good soup.

Piece barbecue — Build a barbecue fire as per page 31. Let the fire burn to coals. Meanwhile, prepare the fish and cut the flesh

41

into 3" square pieces. Erect a single pole rack as explained on page 24. Then thread the halibut squares on iron wood spits or metal skewers.

When the fire is glowing coals, lay the spits at an angle over the fire, with the tips on the rack and the bases approximately 2' from the coals. Sear the flesh side until it is a golden brown. Halibut is a heavy-fleshed, relatively dry fish, so it is important to cook it thoroughly without overdrying.

Turn the fish to the flesh side and allow it to cook for about 30 minutes. It will not drip, as will salmon, to indicate its degree of doneness, so it must be watched closely. After 30 minutes, turn the fish to the skin side and cook for about 10 minutes. Then remove a square to test. The fish is done if it slides readily from the spit and is flaky throughout. If it is not done, return it to the fire for a few more minutes and then test again.

Imu — A whole halibut is rather large to cook with the imu method. It would require a very large fire and take several hours to cook. The finished product would be an achievement on the same level as that produced in the western steer barbecue. Usually halibut roasts of 5 or 6 pounds were used with this method.

Build a fire following directions on page 29. Pick leaves — iron wood is preferred, or maple leaves, or ferns — in which to wrap the fish. Gather green, sand-free seaweed to lay underneath and on top.

Salt and pepper the fish, if you wish, and squeeze some lemon juice in the cavity, or leave natural, Indian fashion. Wrap the fish in the leaves.

When the fire has burned to coals, remove most of the rocks and some of the coals, lay the seaweed on the remaining rocks, place the leaf-wrapped fish on top, and add the rest of the seaweed. Heap gravel over all. Mark the area well so that no unwary walker suffers burned feet.

For a 5-pound roast, allow the fish to cook for an hour. Then open the pit, remove a bit of the seaweed, and test for doneness with a barbecue fork or pointed stick. If the flesh flakes easily to the bone, the fish is done. If not, re-cover the fish and allow another 15 minutes of cooking.

When it is cooked, remove the fish by means of 2 sticks or spatulas. When the wrappings are taken away, the skin may come off, too. This is fine. Serve the fish immediately, while it is steaming hot.

Drying halibut — Cut the halibut flesh into thin strips about ¼" thick and perhaps ½" wide. Hang these in a very warm, dry place where the air can circulate. Be sure they are not touching each other. If it is a hot day, the sun can do the work. If it is not, place the fish near a stove or beside an open fireplace, but not near enough to cook. The objective is drying only. Halibut wasn't smoked — just dried.

The Indians ate the dried halibut as a jerky, reconstituted it by simmering it a few minutes in water, or made it into a chowder.

Flounder and Sole

Flounder and sole are little brothers of the halibut, but while the halibut is thick and meaty, these smaller fish are very flat and produce but one thin fillet per fish. Sole, however, is very tasty and worth the effort to bone it out and cook it on a split-pole rack. It is too thin to skewer on a spit and too small to merit an imu.

Flounder has another drawback. Its skin is extremely rich in iodine. Cooked with the skin on, flounder has a very objectionable taste. It is delicious when skinned, but this is a difficult process. Therefore, flounder was used only when no other fish was available.

For barbecuing sole or flounder, follow the same procedure outlined for small cod on page 40.

Herring and Smelt

When they are spawning, herring and smelt arrive in the bays and estuaries along Puget Sound in great numbers, even today. In the past, before commercial fisheries began to take their toll, the runs must have been prodigious. All the Indian fishermen needed to do was to rake the small silver fish into their canoes.

It was up to the women to process this mountain of fish, and they did so with a minimum of fuss and bother. The fish were not cleaned. Twisted inner cedar bark was threaded through their gills and they were hung to dry and smoke. When the dried fish was served the following winter, it was up to the consumer to eat the flesh and avoid the entrails, if he so desired. Actually, it wasn't so bad - our sardines of today are processed without gutting and we accept them without any fuss.

The smoking process is the same as for salmon. Alder wood is preferred. Hang the strings of fish high enough above the smoke to dry them without cooking. When the fish were thoroughly dry, hard as leather, and half the original size, the Indians placed them in airtight baskets and stored them for winter. Today, hard-smoked herring, wrapped in plastic wrap to keep out dampness, will keep for several months. Soft-smoked herring should be refrigerated, as should all lightly smoked meat and fish.

In the winter, the Indians ate the smoked herring as is, tossed it into a chowder, or boiled it to soften the fish. The taste is similar to kippered herring of British fame.

Herring roe — In the spring, before these small fish arrived at the beaches to spawn, Indians would intertwine cedar branches and lay them in the water. The mothers-to-be found these nurseries particularly to their liking and obliged by depositing their egg masses on the lacy branches. Later, the branches were gathered and laid over smoke fires to cure the eggs. The resultant delicacies were eaten on the spot. Whatever was left was stored in tight baskets for another day.

During the spring spawning season, herring, smelt, and grunion are still available along the gravel beaches of Puget Sound and other inland waters of the coast. Some fanciers dip them from the shallow water or even scoop them from the beaches at night when the fish make a run to the shore to deposit their eggs. At this time, their fat bodies are literally bursting with roe.

Then, too, fresh-caught fish of these varieties are available at fish markets during the spring season. They are sold before cleaning at a time when many of the fish are pregnant. So, if you are a lover of small fish, there is no reason why you shouldn't have the opportunity to try Indian caviar.

To prepare the roe, open the fish carefully, cutting with scissors from the anus to the head. Gently lift out the roe, being careful not to disturb the delicate membrane in which it is sheathed. Sprinkle the roe with water and lemon juice immediately. Salt lightly. When all the fish have been cleaned, package the roe in plastic wrap, sealing it airtight. Refrigerate or freeze it until it is used.

To smoke the roe, you will need to improvise a rack. A piece of screen laid over a metal rack is ideal for this purpose. Any rack will do; try a refrigerator shelf, oven rack, or barbecue grill. Place the rack on a wooden rack framework as described on page 26.

Build a smoke fire under the rack following directions on page 32. Keep the fire tiny to allow smoke only. When smoke is pouring

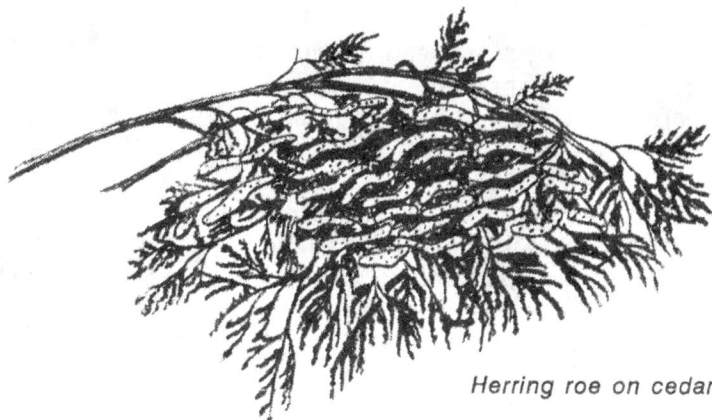

Herring roe on cedar branch

out, lay the eggs on the rack. Screen the fire as necessary to keep the smoke circulating about the eggs. After 3 hours, check the roe. It is done when it is firm to the touch and brown in color. it will smell decidedly smoky.

To store, seal the roe in a jar and/or refrigerate.

Skates and Rays

These strange, flat fish, relatives to the shark, were caught and relished by the Coast Indians. The fish were cleaned by making an incision on the bottom side and removing the entrails. Since they are quite flat, they were not boned out, but were cooked whole. Large skates and rays were ideally cooked in an imu or pit oven along with clams, oysters, moon snails, and other shellfish. Smaller fish were barbecued on a rack.

Barbecue method — Build a barbecue fire following directions on page 31. While the fire is burning to coals, build a rack according to directions on page 26. Use iron wood for the rack, since the barbecue time will be relatively long and a softer wood might wilt or burn under the heat.

Place the fish on the rack over the fire of coals. It will not be necessary to sear the fish, since there is no exposed flesh. Cook it on one side until the skin is brown and crusty. Then flip it to the other side using flat sticks. It may take several cooks to accomplish the turning. Brown the other side. Flip back to the original side. Cut through the skin and test for doneness. If the fish is flaky, it is cooked. Skin the fish. The skin should peel back easily. The fish is ready to serve.

45

Imu or pit method — Clean the fish by slitting the abdomen and removing the organs and entrails.

Prepare a fire according to page 29. While the fire is dying down, gather a large pile of clean seaweed. Wrap the fish in a layer of seaweed about 3" thick.

When the fire has burned to coals, scrape out some of the rocks and embers. Place the fish on the remaining rocks and cover it with the rest of the rocks and coals. Put gravel over the fish, heaping it up to about 1' thick. Mark the spot well.

Allow the fish to bake for about 1 hour. Open a small hole in the pit, cut through the seaweed and outer skin, and test for doneness. As with all fish, the flesh should be moist, but flake easily.

To remove the fish from the fire, place flat sticks under it and lift it out. Peel off the skin and serve immediately.

Dogfish

The small, harmless shark commonly called dogfish was eaten by some of the Salish groups. Although not so highly valued as salmon or halibut, it was nutritious and plentiful. Salish cooks found that the heavy, pure white flesh could be prepared in a number of ways, including fish soup. Since the shark has no bones, only a strong cartilage that softens during cooking, the flesh was unusually easy to prepare.

Clean the shark. Remove the head, fins, and tail. It is advisable to skin the shark before cooking, since it has a rather strong iodine and ammonia taste which is objectionable to some. Skinning is difficult, requiring a sharp knife and lots of tenacity. If equipment is available, parboil the fish for a few minutes to loosen the skin. The Indians did not throw the skin away. It was highly prized for its abrasive quality. Carvers used it to give wood a smooth, highly polished finish.

As a concession to modern palates, season the shark inside and out with salt, pepper, and lemon juice. Let the fish sit for a few minutes to absorb the flavors.

Piece barbecue — Build a fire as indicated on page 31. Let the fire burn to coals. While waiting, prepare the fish by cutting it into 3" squares. Erect racks as described on page 24 and use iron wood spits made according to directions on page 24. Thread the fish onto the spits.

Lay the spits over the coals with the tips on the racks. Sear the fish on one side and then the other until it is golden brown. The flesh is relatively dry, so be careful not to overcook. Cook the fish about 15 minutes to a side. Test for doneness by flaking with a fork. The flesh should be tender and very white.

Imu or pit method — Build a fire according to directions on page 29. Gather a large quantity of fresh, green seaweed that is sand free. If they are available, pick enough iron wood leaves to cover the shark, or substitute ferns or maple leaves.

Wrap the fish in the leaves. They will impart a delicious, subtle flavor. For today's palate, salt, pepper, and lemon juice might be helpful, or try sliced lemon laid into the body cavity.

When the fire has burned to coals, scrape some of the rocks and coals from the fire. Place the leaf-wrapped fish on the coals and cover it with seaweed. Heap the rest of the rocks and coals on top and cover all with gravel. Mark the spot.

Allow the shark to bake for 1½ hours. Open the pit and cut through the seaweed to check the flesh. The fish is cooked if a fork will easily pierce to the center. Remove the fish from the pit and serve immediately.

Fish Chowder

Except for the viscera, no edible part of the fish was thrown away. Excellent chowders were made from the head and backbones of fish. Since the Indians cut out the backbone before cooking or drying their fish, there was some flesh adhering to it. They relished the heads, finding the meat succulent and tasty. These went into soups along with whatever vegetables were available. Dried seaweed was often added, both for its salt content and as a thickener. When boiled, the seaweed became jellylike.

Shellfish 6

EQUAL IN IMPORTANCE to the salmon, clams and other shellfish were staples in the Coast Salish menu. Clams, oysters, mussels, whelks, moon snails, barnacles, limpets, sea urchins, and crabs were plentiful along the beaches.

It was women's work to gather and prepare them for immediate consumption or to preserve them for winter use. A woman's prestige was enhanced by her ability to dig copious amounts of clams and to dry and smoke vast stores of them for the winter.

The Coast Salish attached great importance to all forms of life as fellow beings. They believed clams were people who lived in villages under the sea. The form they assumed as clams was temporary and designed to assist the Indians by providing them with food. Once the clam was consumed, it would return to its own people. An old legend illustrates the Indian philosophy:

"There was once an Indian princess named Ay a mat who lived with her parents in a great longhouse on the shores of Puget Sound. She was very unhappy. As was the custom among families of high rank, when girls reached the age of puberty they were compelled to stay in a separate part of the house. Ay a mat was now on the brink of womanhood and she had been placed in confinement. She could no longer play with other children. She could no longer run free as the birds, swift as the deer. Life was very dull for her and she longed to escape.

"One day her parents were called away to an Indian gathering and she was left alone in her quarters. 'Stay where you are,' they commanded. 'Don't let anything lure you away.' She fully intended to obey her parents, but the temptation to seek playmates was too great.

"'This is the only chance I'll have,' she thought. She went outside and to her delight there were other children playing on the beach. The tide was going out. Someone said, 'Let's get some clams.'

"Ay a mat thought that would be fun, so she ran out onto the sandy flats and joined them. Soon they were digging horse clams and shrieking with joy when they pulled out a big one.

"The tide changed and began to come in. Noticing the incoming rivulets, the children drifted toward the shore. But Ay a mat had found a huge clam hole, bigger than any she had ever seen before. She kept digging, until at last, if she lay on her stomach and reached far down into the hole, she could feel the giant clam. As her fingers groped for a hold on it, the clamshell closed tightly on her thumb. Try as she would, she could not wrench free, nor could she drag the clam to the surface.

"The other children called, but she could not come. The water crept closer and closer to her, and finally it rose over her head.

"This was no ordinary clam, just as Ay a mat was no ordinary girl. Strangely, she found that she could breathe under water. When the tide came in full, the clam took her to a village underneath the sea where the clam people lived. There she spent the rest of her life, becoming more and more like the clam people.

"But she longed for her own people. As a special favor, when she had pleased them, the clam people allowed Ay a mat to travel to the surface of the water. There she could see her village at a distance and perhaps watch the people as they paddled across the bay in their canoes.

"One day, when a terrible storm was raging, Ay a mat begged her captors to let her swim to the surface. 'My people may be in danger. Perhaps I can help them,' she said.

"The clam people allowed her to go. But they warned her that she was one of them now, that no one would recognize her or understand her words.

"When Ay a mat reached the surface, she saw a canoe foundering. Immediately she recognized her own parents and tried to call to them, but the only sound she could make was like the shrieking of the wind.

"'What was that?' her mother asked. 'In a strange way, it sounded to me like Ay a mat was calling to us.'

"'It is only the wind,' her father said. 'Use your canoe bailer. The canoe is taking water faster than we can bail it out!'

"'What is that?' her mother asked again. 'See over there? It makes me think of Ay a mat.'

"'It's only a seal,' her father said, 'or a strange sea creature.'

"'It is gesturing,' cried her mother. 'See the waters are becoming calmer.'

"'Then it must be a spirit of the sea come to help us,' the father answered.

"'No,' her mother answered. 'That is Ay a mat come to save us.'

"And so," the legend continues, "whenever there is a storm, the Indian maiden rises from the sea to warn the people and to help them if they are in danger."

Clams

Finding and digging clams — Clams were found in such abundance on Puget Sound beaches that much of a woman's time was spent digging and processing them. When the clam season came, all else was laid aside. Veritable mountains of clams were dug. Browsing through kitchen middens, the garbage dumps of Indian villages, one finds literally tons of clamshells. All sorts of clams were taken, including steamer or littlenecks, butter, cockles, and horse clams.

Horse clams *(Tresus capax):* Far out on beaches, at the lowest tides, Indian women sought giant horse clams. These large bivalves usually sit several feet under the sand, with their long, rubbery necks extended so that the siphons lay at or just below the surface. This feature, plus the fact that they are constantly processing seawater through their systems to extract nourishment, makes them easy to find. Look for large holes or depressions in the sand. Occasionally, you will see the siphon, itself, laying exposed, or just protruding, looking crusty and unappetizing. But watch out for a shower of recycled seawater that can arch over your head and drench you. These clams feel the vibration of your footsteps. They become alarmed and draw down their necks, ejecting a stream of water with great force. It is part of the excitement of digging horse clams and nothing to worry about.

Indian women dug horse clams with specially designed "digging sticks" made from hardwood such as maple or cherry. They were long and slender with a slight scoop at the end. To make them

Cockle
(Clinocardium nuttallii)

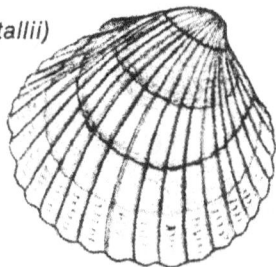

Horse clam
(Tresus capax)

50

Clam basket and digging stick

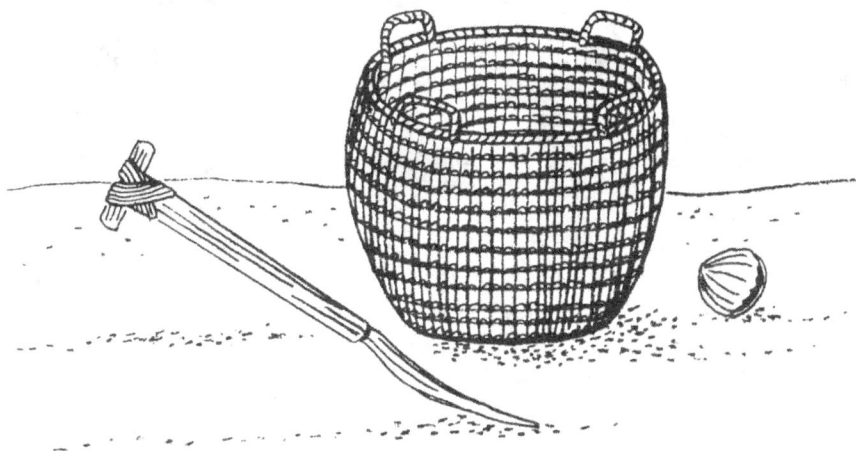

sturdy, the tips were fire hardened by exposing them to the heat of a fire. The wood was not burned, but charred slightly. Today, we use specially designed shovels, called "clam guns," which are long and tapered.

The trick for getting horse clams is to sneak up on them. Walk softly. When you have sighted a hole or cluster, dig down about 1' away from the hole so as not to crush the shell. Dig as rapidly as possible. It becomes a contest, for the clam not only can pull its neck down two feet to its body in a matter of seconds, but it can also use its muscular foot to dig itself rapidly into the sand. You are in the vicinity of the clam when your hole is several feet deep and probably filled with seawater.

Some diggers lie flat and thrust their arms in, up to the shoulder, seeking the clam. Others rely on the shovel to bring it up. However it is done, one good-sized horse clam is worth the effort, for it, alone, will make a respectable chowder.

Cockles *(Clinocardium nuttallii):* As if to make up for the difficulty in obtaining horse clams, nature, or Gha-hals as the Indians would say, created cockles. These heart-shaped clams are found from low tide to the intertidal area, just beneath the surface of sandy beaches or even lying exposed in tidepools. Look for ridges in the sand. The clam prefers to sit upright with the lips of its shell just under the sand. This angle creates a slight mound with an abrupt break where the shell is open to let the siphon bring in food. Nature has equipped it with a relatively short neck, often its undoing.

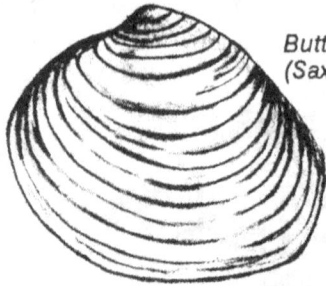

Butter clam
(Saxidomus giganteus)

Littleneck clam
(Protothaca staminea)

The people relished the cockle, often eating it raw. It has a very large, strong foot which is tough, but sweet tasting. Today, we resort to the food grinder and a chowder recipe.

Butter clams *(Saxidomus giganteus):* Indian women prized butter clams above all others. Kitchen middens are full of butter clam shells. The clams are tender enough to be steamed and eaten plain. They are large enough to be worth the effort of digging them, and plentiful enough to fill a bucket in a short time. They are found closer to shore than the cockles, and so are available more often. Butter clams seem to like beaches of gravel and sand. They lie 6" to 1' beneath the surface, and can be dug with a stick or a trowel.

Butters were steamed in pits and eaten immediately or smoked for winter storage. Today, we enjoy these gourmet treats in the same way the Salish did, steamed or in chowders.

Steamers or littlenecks *(Protothaca staminea):* Right at the water's edge, hidden away in gravel bars, the women found the most delectable of Puget Sound clams, the littleneck. These small clams, measuring no more than 2" when mature, were steamed and eaten around the pit as a treat.

Clam lovers today will find a bonus when they go after steamers. They are local clams which can be identified by their designs which resemble the designs used on Indian baskets. There are also Manilla steamers which are an introduced variety. These clams occur in brilliant colors, including yellows, blacks, and other shades.

Digging steamers is a little tricky and requires a knowledge of their habits. The steamers prefer gravel and sand beaches and can stand long exposure to the sun. They are found at approximately the mean tideline. Some diggers use a small rake, others use a claw or hoe, or even a hand trowel. Whatever you choose, the digging will be easy work, but it requires patience.

Steamers live just under the surface of the beach, about 3" down, resting in an up-and-down position. They resemble a stone, at first glance, particularly if the beach is muddy or of a clay composition. The best procedure is to begin a shallow excavation, scraping the gravel from the sides and sluicing the clams through the water at the bottom of the hole. Some clammers rake the clams through and up the other side of the excavation, separating them from the gravel. Others prefer to pick the clams from their positions as they are exposed by the digging. Make sure your clams are of legal size. The tiny ones are too small to even taste.

When you are digging clams, fill in the holes and level the beach when you are through. Each time you dig, you are disturbing entire ecosystems and upsetting the delicate balance on the beach. To minimize the impact of your efforts, leave the beach the way you found it.

Cleaning clams — Indian women developed an ingenious way to clean clams. They took advantage of the action of the tides to do their work for them. Clams were collected in open mesh baskets of twined cedar bark. The baskets were placed in the water to let the flowing of the incoming tide wash the sand and mud from their contents. It didn't matter if the clams remained several days, since they would feed and be cleansed during that time.

Horse clams were cleaned on the beach. The inedible parts such as the tip of the siphon, the gills, and the stomach were left to feed other sea creatures. Other varieties of clams were cooked without further cleaning, according to the recipes given later.

Certain parts of a clam are more subject to the toxic poisoning known as red tide. As a safety measure, it is wise to clean clams before eating, removing the tip of the siphon and the gills, since these are the parts where toxins tend to concentrate. This can be done after steaming, if desired. Littlenecks are so small that cleaning them is impractical. If there is any danger of a red tide, the safest thing is not to eat them at all.

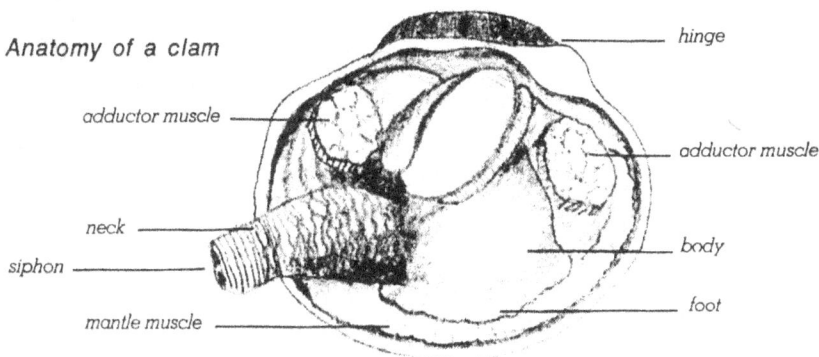

Anatomy of a clam

hinge

adductor muscle

adductor muscle

neck

body

siphon

foot

mantle muscle

Recipes

Clam chowder from dried clams — Most clam chowders were prepared in winter, using dried, powdered clams. Clams were pulverized with mortar and pestle and simmered in boxes or baskets of water using the hot rocks method. Indian vegetables such as dried seaweed and wild onions were added to the chowder.

Pound the clams to a fine powder, or use a meat grinder with a fine blade, and cut the vegetables into small pieces. Add the ingredients to water in a basket or pot. The amount of water will depend on the volume of food used. The Indian cooks did not measure, but cooked by instinct. Fill the cooking pot no more than half full and simmer with the hot rocks method as described on page 27. Allow the chowder to cook for about 20 minutes or until the vegetables are tender.

After the advent of the white man, Indian women still went about their business of gathering and drying clams, but they now had additional ingredients to use in making their soups and stews. Potatoes, onions, carrots, celery, salt and pepper, and bacon fat and pieces were ingredients that the Indians, themselves, found to their liking.

Clam chowder from fresh clams — If an Indian cook was preparing a stew from fresh ingredients, she might well put in whatever was available, which certainly included clams. The process was the same as for dried clam chowder. A dozen fresh butter clams or two dozen steamers will make a good chowder. One or two horse clams will provide the same amount of meat. To prepare the horse clam, remove the stomach portion, skin the neck, and be sure that no sand remains. Pound the clam thoroughly. It will shred into bits and pieces and become quite slimy. Cook as for dried clam chowder.

Steamed clams — Steamer and butter clams were prepared by steaming them in a pit. Truly the original clambake was the time-honored Indian method. Often other food, such as the tender shoots of salmonberries, the new fern growth called fiddleheads, or the hearts of cattails were bundled together and tied with inner cedar bark to be added to the imu.

Wash the clams in the sea. The old method of using open mesh baskets may be forever gone in favor of the present-day use of open mesh onion sacks. Allow the water to wash surface sand from the shells.

While the sacks are swishing, gather a large quantity of fresh, green seaweed. Build an imu fire as described on page 29. Scrape out the coals and place a heavy layer of seaweed on the hot rocks. Lay the clams on the seaweed, cover them with another layer of seaweed, and heap sand and beach gravel over it all. Mark the area well.

Allow the clams to steam for about ½ hour. Poke a hole through the sand and seaweed and examine several clams. If the shells have opened, they are done. If the shells are not open, replace the seaweed and allow the clams to steam another 10 minutes. Test again.

To remove the clams, carefully scrape away all the gravel. Lift off the seaweed, watching that no sand sifts down into the clams below. When the clams are exposed, remove them to serving dishes with tongs. Take care that the clams do not drop out of the shells when you are handling them.

Serve in the shells. The Indians passed around about a bowl of fish oil in which to dip the clams. Today, we often use drawn butter for the same purpose.

Barbecued clams — Prepare a barbecue fire on the beach in the manner that is described on page 31. While the fire is burning down to coals, skewer the clams on iron wood spits so that they cover the upper foot of the spit. When the coals are right, set one end of the spit into the ground at an angle over the fire. Cooking time is about 10 minutes for small clams and 20 minutes for large ones.

Curing clams for winter — Barbecued and steamed clams were dried and smoked for the winter. They were processed into hard pellets that were stored in tightly covered storage baskets. The people soaked and simmered the clams before use. The Indians removed barbecued clams from the spits and threaded cedar bark string through the skewer holes to tie the clams together for drying on a rack.

Place the clams on a rack in the sun to dry or, in the event of a cool day, over a smoky fire to cure. This process could take several days, depending on the weather and the fire. Take great care not to overheat the clams or they will cook rather than cure and dry. Care must also be taken to see that the clams dry evenly and relatively quickly, so that they do not mold.

Place serving-sized portions in paper bags (to keep out the light) and then into sealed plastic bags. A number of these portions may be sealed into a larger plastic bag and stored at room temperature. Soft-smoked or soft-cured meats or fish should be kept under refrigeration.

Oysters

Today, the beaches along Puget Sound abound in large, succulent oysters. Such was not always the case. In the days when the Indians owned the fishing and hunting areas, there were just two varieties of oyster, the Olympia oyster and the rock oyster. Both were delicious, but they were not abundant and they were difficult to break from the rocks.

Oysters were not smoked for winter use, probably because their soft bodies did not dry properly for storage. They were baked in a pit, as were clams, or they were barbecued directly on the coals of a fire.

Barbecue method — Build a beach fire with alder, cherry, maple, or any slow-burning wood. Let it burn to glowing coals. Place the oysters on the coals. Make sure that all are tightly closed. The oysters will sputter and steam. When they are baked, the shells will open. Eat immediately, as is, from the halfshell.

Steaming method — Build a pit fire as shown on page 29. Place a layer of seaweed on the coals, lay the oysters on the seaweed, and cover them with more seaweed. Heap rocks and gravel on top to a depth of 1' or more and mark the spot. Allow the imu to remain for up to 1 hour. Test for doneness by digging into one corner of the pit. Use tongs to remove an oyster. The oyster is done if the shell is open.

Crabs

Crabs are shallow water dwellers found in large numbers in bays where eelgrass grows. They were greatly enjoyed by the Salish people. They still are today. The Dungeness crab, considered by many to be the tastiest of all the crabs, grew to a huge size and was easily taken. The people speared them from their canoes or picked them from under the eelgrass. The crab was stunned by a sharp rap on the carapace just behind the eyes, the back was ripped off, and the insides removed.

Barbecued crab — Erect a rack of green iron wood over a bed of coals. See directions on page 26. Lay the cleaned crabs on the rack and barbecue for about ½ hour. Turn the crabs occasionally to ensure even cooking. Test for doneness by removing a leg. If the flesh inside is firm and free from the shell, it is cooked.

Steamed crab — Crabs, like other forms of shellfish, can be baked in a pit. Since their cooking time is the same as that of oysters and clams, you can easily cook them in the same pit, as a shore dinner. Build a fire as shown on page 29. Place a heavy layer of seaweed on the coals. Lay the crabs on the seaweed and cover them with another seaweed layer. Heap sand and gravel on top to a depth of 1'. Mark the spot. Open the pit in ½ hour to test for doneness. Cook as long as necessary. The crab meat should be firm and free from the shell.

Crab

Meat

Venison

Deer were actively hunted for their meat. Not only were they sought by bow and arrow, but huge nets were also erected across known deer paths to catch the wary animals as they fled from noise created by hunters.

Venison was a welcome change from the normal fish diet of the people. They employed all three cooking methods, boiling, roasting, and barbecuing, depending on the time and circumstances. Boiling was quick and sure, but added nothing to the taste or texture of the venison. Barbecuing was relatively easy, too, provided there was time for a properly built and aged fire. Roasting, on the other hand, took the best part of a day and required a large pit and a great deal of wood. But the roasted results were so superior that it was usually considered worth the effort.

Boiling method — Prepare a fire according to directions on page 30. Heat the rocks and place them in a pot to boil the water. Add venison chunks. The water should just cover the meat. Rotate the hot rocks until the meat is cooked. Vegetables, such as wild onions, greens, or tender shoots can be added to make a stew.

Spit barbecue method — Build a fire according to directions on page 31. Skewer serving-sized portions of venison on spits. Set the spits into the ground beside the fire so that the meat is at an angle over the coals. If you desire, place shells below the meat to catch the juices as they drop.

Roasting method — Directions for a pit or imu fire are found on page 29. While the fire is burning down to a bed of coals, gather armloads of bracken fern tops. Rake up a pile of green, wet seaweed—the ribbon type is best. Skin the deer and clean it thoroughly. It is possible to roast a whole deer using the pit method, but this is impractical. You may wish to butcher the meat into 3-pound pieces for a more manageable imu bake.

Wrap the meat pieces individually in several layers of bracken or sword fern leaves. When the fire has been reduced to about 3" of glowing coals, place a layer of seaweed about 1" thick on the coals. Quickly lay the meat bundles on the seaweed. Add more seaweed to cover and heap several feet of beach gravel over all. Mark the spot. Allow the imu to remain for 5 or 6 hours. Open the pit and remove one of the bundles. Test for doneness. If it is not done, return it and wait another hour or so.

If a whole deer is to be roasted, dig a huge pit and prepare a very deep bed of coals. Place a thick layer of seaweed on the coals and layer ferns on top. Deposit the prepared deer on this. Cover the deer with more ferns and place another layer of seaweed around and on top of it. Finally, cover the whole thing with a thick layer of beach gravel and mark the spot. Mound it up several feet. Open the pit after 10 hours and test.

Dried venison — The Coast Salish dried venison into jerky. It was cut into thin strips and dried in the summer sun. If you try to dry the meat, take it inside at night to prevent dew from moistening it. If the sun fails to shine, dry the meat near an inside heat source. When the venison was thoroughly dried, the Indians stored it in airtight baskets. Today, store the meat in airtight plastic bags at room temperature.

Bear

The Coast Salish people were water oriented. They seldom ventured more than a mile or so up the rivers unless it was absolutely necessary. Their association with the black bear was limited to those hunting and berrying expeditions that led them beyond their normal range, up the rivers, and into the mountains.

For those groups who utilized bear product, the killing of a bear was a happy occasion. The pelt was valued as a blanket or robe, the claws became ornaments, the teeth were used for jewelry, and the flesh was eaten with gusto.

Another bonus was bear grease. It was caught in clamshells placed below the cooking meat and used much as we use butter and mayonnaise today.

Bear meat was usually barbecued in chunks, either roasting it on iron wood spits or by laying the meat on racks of iron wood raised over a hot-coals fire. Because of its rare appearances in the people's diet, and its oily quality, bear meat was a prized delicacy. It was the makings of a feast.

Spit barbecue method — Build a fire according to the directions on page 31. Cut the bear meat into ½-pound servings and skewer the meat on spits. Place the meat at an angle to the fire, but not too close, since the aim here is to allow the fat to run out and not to sear the meat. Cook the meat slowly, turning it frequently to cook all sides. You may wish to puncture the meat occasionally to encourage the fat to drip. You may wish to catch the fat in clamshells for future use. Test the doneness. Bear is subject to trichinosis, as is pork, so cook very thoroughly.

Large rack method — The rack method is tricky, since dripping fat will cause the fire to flare and sputter. Place the rack well above the coals so there is no chance of it catching fire. Directions for rack cookery are found on page 26. Cut the meat into serving-sized pieces and turn frequently until done.

Small animals

Kitchen middens are filled with the bones of small animals. Lying among the vast heaps of decaying clamshells are found the bones of rabbits, squirrels, fox, beaver, and perhaps, sea otters, land otters, and mink. According to elderly Indian women, most of the small animals found their way into soups and stews. However, some were barbecued whole on a spit that was shoved through the cavity left when the entrails were removed and into the base of the skull. Rabbits, in particular, were enjoyed barbecued; the results were very tasty.

Wild animal stew — Prepare a fire according to directions on page 30. Heat rocks, if you plan to be truly authentic in your effort, otherwise place several cups of water in a kettle and set it to heat on rocks beside a fire. Place water in your cooking pot or box to the depth of about 6". Add small pieces of meat. Rotate the rocks between the water and the fire to keep the water simmering. When the meat is nearly done, 1 hour or so, add vegetables. Goose foot, lamb's quarters, glasswort, cow parsnip, wapato, and fiddleheads might be included. See the chapter on vegetables to aid identification.

Wild animal soup — Indian soups were usually broths made from fish, meat, or fowl available at a given time. Dried seaweed was often added to give savor to the soup and to add very necessary vitamins and minerals. Follow the directions for stew, increasing the amount of water and eliminating the vegetables, except for cow parsnip or onions which add greatly to the flavor. See page 86 for instructions on edible seaweed and the method for drying it.

Ducks and Geese

In the spring and again late in the fall, the air was filled with the whirring of wings and the almost deafening sound of thousands of ducks and brant as they passed over coastal villages on their yearly migration route. It was the signal for the hunter to erect and tend his duck nets. These nets, placed high in the air near known resting and feeding stops, would snare hundreds of startled ducks as they wheeled into the air upon the approach of hunters.

The people relished duck. Even today, they serve a special duck soup upon the occasion of a wedding, a naming, or other important activity. Duck was served a number of ways including soup, stew, barbecue, and roast.

Duck soup and stew — These were prepared following the same directions as wild animal soup and stew found on page 60. Plunge the birds into boiling water for easier plucking.

Barbecue method — Barbecued duck presented problems because of the difficulty in removing the pinfeathers. This was a

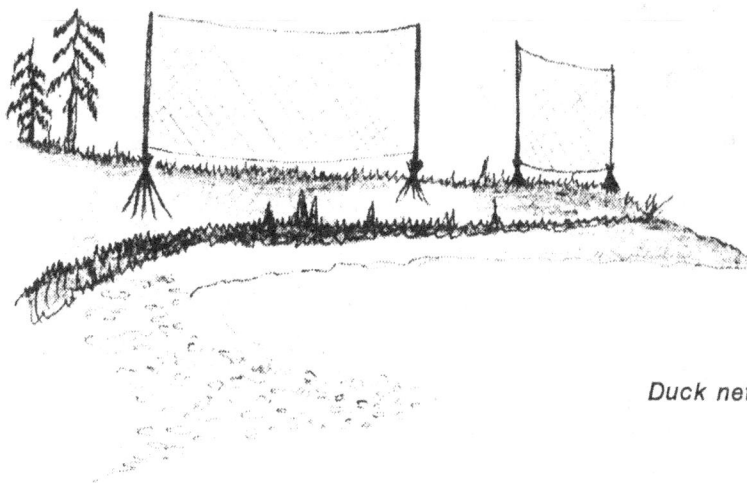

Duck nets

particular problem if many ducks needed to be prepared and served at one time. The time required for duck plucking could be enormous. To meet this problem, the ingenious Salish cooks invented a special method for cooking ducks.

Clean the duck with the head and feathers intact. When the barbecue fire is ready (see page 31) impale the ducks on iron wood spits. Shove the spit into the duck's bill and down its throat. Push the spit into the ground so that the duck hangs beside and over the coals.

Rotate the spit to change the position of the duck throughout cooking. The feathers will singe and perhaps even burn off, but it does not matter one way or the other. Test for doneness by trying to take off the legs and wings. The duck is fully cooked if these are loose and move freely. When the duck is cooked, remove it from the fire and peel the skin away. It will come loose: feathers, pinfeathers, and all.

Baked method — Baked duck was a classic example of Salish invention. Indian women say that their great-grandmothers prepared roast duck with all the juices intact and no plucking required.

For this method, clay was used. This presented no problem, for the Pacific Northwest abounds in a good quality clay, capable of being fired at a relatively low temperature. The Indians were aware of the possibilities of clay, even though they did not use it to make pottery.

The proper type of clay is still available today. Blue gray in color, it is found where streams cut into their bank or along beaches where bluffs have eroded away. If found in an area where there has been a recent washout, the clay is pure enough to be easily worked.

Dig out some clay. If it is soft already, just squish it in your hands a bit, and then plaster it all over the cleaned, unplucked duck. The clay should be at least 1" thick, no thicker than 1½". Lay the clay-covered bird aside to dry.

Build a pit fire according to directions on page 29. Lay the clay-coated duck on the coals. Cover the pit with gravel and let it remain undisturbed for about 4 hours. Mark the spot.

Open the pit and use tongs or a stick to roll the duck out. The clay will be fired hard. Let it cool for 15 minutes or more. Break the clay shell and begin to pull it away from the duck. The skin and feathers will come away with the clay, leaving a clean, tasty duck for you to eat.

Other birds

Brant, herons, sea gulls, and other northwest coast birds were also used for food. Brant were treated in the same way as ducks, while the rest usually ended up in the stewpot.

Seal

Seals were valued for the oil that was obtained from their thick layers of fat. This was cut away from the meat, rendered into oil, and stored for use as an accompaniment to dried food in the winter time.

Seal meat was eaten, but it was not relished as highly as venison or bear. Indians, today, suggest that it was either roasted or boiled for a very long time, since the meat is tough.

The seal was cut into roasts of about 3 pounds, the thick layers of fat were removed, and the meat was boiled until it was reasonably tender, using the hot rocks method. Vegetables were added toward the end of the cooking time. Alternatively, the meat was roasted in a pit for at least 4 hours.

Vegetables  8

IT IS A POPULAR BELIEF that the Coast Salish Indians were fish eaters and had little use for vegetables. This is not true. While they did not practice agriculture to the extent of plowing land and planting crops, they did own and maintain, on a family basis, land that produced vegetables.

Camas fields, for example, were carefully utilized so that the camas continued to grow and multiply while providing an ample supply of this favorite food. When fern roots were taken, the patches were never cleaned out; they were thinned in a manner which allowed the remaining ferns to grow.

The people enjoyed a variety of vegetables, including roots, stems, and leaves. They were eaten fresh, preserved for winter, and cooked in a variety of methods. Small wild potatoes were baked or added to stews. Camas, cattail roots, and a variety of fern roots were baked to soften. In the spring there was an abundance of greens to choose from, including salmonberry shoots, cattail hearts, miner's lettuce, lamb's quarters, nettle, and cow parsnip. In the fall, the people harvested wild rice from the marshy floodplains of the rivers.

With all this natural bounty, the Coast Indians dined well on the food they gathered from the meadows, woods, and riverbanks.

Bulbs, Roots, and Tubers

Camas *(Camassia quamash)* — Camas was, by far, the most valued vegetable, and it figured in much of the people's cookery. When the family groups visited the camas fields, the women spent hundreds of backbreaking hours digging the small onionlike bulbs with specially designed digging sticks. They carefully peeled back the sod in squares and removed the larger bulbs from under the dirt. The smaller bulblets were left undisturbed to thrive and grow.

The camas were baked on the spot in giant imu pits. See directions on page 29. While the fire was heating the rocks and the ground beneath it, the women washed the bulbs, swishing them through seawater until they were clean.

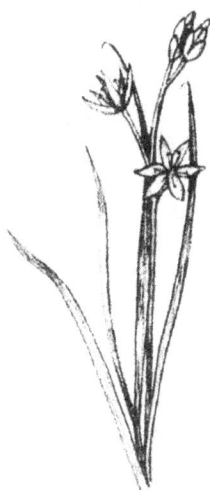

Camas
(Camassia quamash)

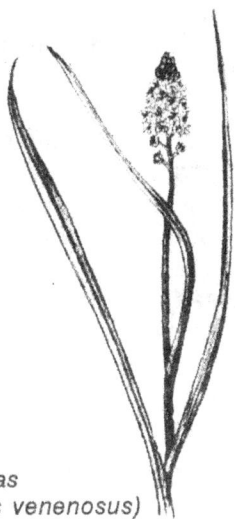

Death camas
(Zygadenus venenosus)

The embers were scraped to one side of the pit and it was lined with iron wood leaves. Quickly, the camas were dropped onto the leaves and covered with a second leaf layer. Heated rocks and embers were scraped back on top and the whole pit was covered with gravel. The pit remained undisturbed for twenty-four hours.

The pit fires burned continuously during the processing periods. They were tended by the older women, who rotated their duties between heating rocks, filling the pits with camas, and removing the cooked food. After cooking, the camas were dried whole in the sun and stored in mesh baskets for winter use. Sometimes the soft, moist bulbs were kneaded into loaves and dried and stored.

Two forms of camas grow in meadows and on grassy bluffs on the islands and mainlands of Puget Sound country. The smaller of the two varieties displays stalks of blue lilylike blossoms in late May or early June, while the other blooms several weeks later, producing stalkier and heavier blooms. Their large bulbs are covered with a membranous skin of a brown color and often grow to well over an inch thick. Camas leaves are grasslike.

When digging camas be certain that you are digging true camas and not death camas. Death camas is highly toxic. Unless death camas is in flower, it is difficult to tell the two plants apart; the bulbs and leaves are similar and they occur in the same areas. The best rule is to dig the plants only when they are in flower from May through June. Camas will have flower stems 12" to 20" long with a loose terminal cluster of blue blossoms. Death camas bears cream-colored flowers that are smaller and in a tighter spike.

Bracken fern, lady fern, and cattail roots — The fleshy roots of fern and cattail were staples in the Indian diet. They were roasted in the same manner as the camas, eaten right from the fire, or preserved by pounding and drying for winter use. Roasted bracken fern root has a texture and taste similar to the sweet potato. Pounded and kneaded cattail roots have a taste and texture similar to poi. Chewed raw, fern roots were considered to be remedies for a cough and sore throat.

Wapato *(Sagittaria latifolia)* — Often called Indian potato or arrow leaf, the wapato formed a basic food for some of the Salish groups.

It grows wholly or partially submerged in water or wet mud and is available wherever there are swampy conditions. The Salish people claimed wapato patches by clearing the area of competing growth to gain access to the tubers. Such temporary owners might camp at a wapato site while harvesting during October and November. Since the tubers lay under the water, the work was done by canoe, pulling the roots from a kneeling position, or as an alternative, by wading in the water and dislodging the tubers with the toes. Wapato tubers kept for several months if left unwashed in the raw

*Wapato
(Sagittaria latifolia)*

*Bracken
(Pteridium aquilinum)*

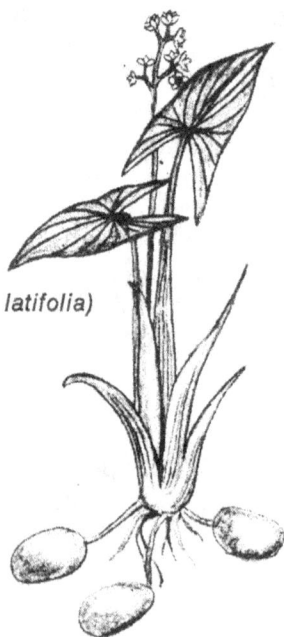

66

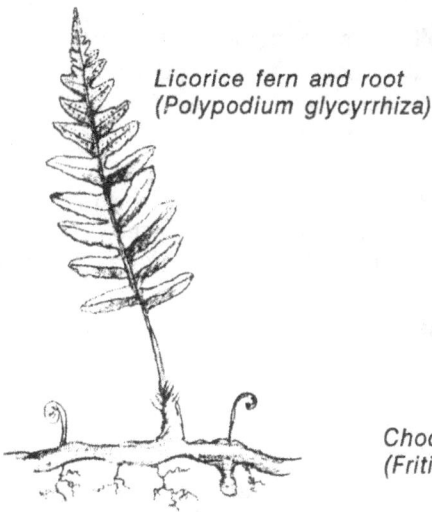

Licorice fern and root
(Polypodium glycyrrhiza)

Chocolate lily
(Fritillaria lanceolata)

state. They were stored and cooked as needed by baking in hot ashes. The wapato resembles the potato in texture, but has a sweeter taste.

Chocolate lily *(Fritillaria lanceolata)* — This lovely member of the lily family grows on meadows and grassy bluffs, often near camas beds. Having a chocolate brown flower, the lily is unique and easily recognized. It possesses a bell-shaped bulb that is covered with bulblets resembling grains of rice. When these bulbs are steamed in a pit, they become tender and delicate, with a texture similar to rice. Chocolate lilies are not plentiful, so it is suggested that Indian-type conservation be practiced by those who taste its bulb. Dig a square of the sod from underneath, lift it, extract the largest bulbs and leave the rest to grow and multiply by replacing the sod carefully.

Licorice fern *(Polypodium glycyrrhiza)* — This small fern grows on mossy logs or tree trunks in damp areas. It particularly likes old maple trees. Its tender, thickish roots have a licorice flavor that qualify it as a snacking food. Indian children who would not eat were sometimes offered licorice fern as an appetizer. Although the fern roots were available year round, some were dried for convenient use in the winter time.

Water lily *(Nuphar polysepalum)* — The showy water lily, its bright yellow cups adding spots of gaiety to lakes and ponds of the Pacific Northwest, possesses starchy roots that lend themselves to baking or roasting in a pit. Allow considerable time, since the roots are coarse and somewhat woody. After baking for 5 or 6 hours, the roots may be skinned and eaten, shredded and added to stew, or pounded into a flour and stored for later use. The flour was used as a soup thickener or was baked into a type of bread.

The Indians valued water lilies as a tonic for a variety of ailments. Pick the roots of small water lilies, wash them, and break and mash them. Remove the outside bark and mix the mash with moss and the inner bark of the spruce tree. Boil the ingredients for 3½ hours. Drink the liquid as a cure-all.

Skunk cabbage *(Lysichitum americanum)* — Early in the spring, the giant yellow flower of the skunk cabbage brightens dismal swamplands. There is no mistaking this one-of-a-kind plant. It has gigantic bright leaves that are oblong and succulent with deeply impressed veins. Because of its characteristic strong taste, extra treatment is required to make the root, stock, and leaves of the plant palatable.

Wash the roots well. Soak them in water for several days. Change the water frequently. The leaves, too, should be washed in several changes of water. The Indians roasted and dried the root, sometimes grinding it into a flour that was used for a kind of bread or for a soup thickener. The plant's peppery taste will ease after several weeks of storage.

The young leaves are cooked as greens, immediately after they emerge from the ground. The water must be changed several times during the cooking process.

Water lily
(Nuphar polysepalum)

Skunk cabbage
(Lysichitum americanum)

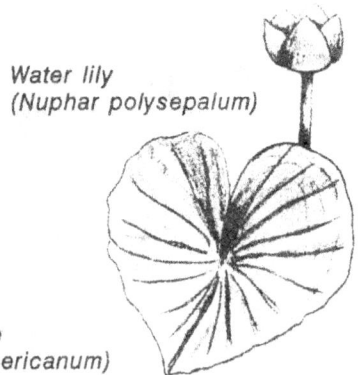

Wild rice

Wild rice, apparently, used to grow in swampy areas along freshwater sloughs. To gather it, the women paddled small, shallow-draft canoes among the ripe rice. They beat the rice into canoes by hitting it with long sticks. The rice was placed on trays and tossed into the air to clean. Afterwards, it was dried in the sun.

The rice was cooked using the hot rocks method. Build a fire according to instructions on page 30. Place several cups of water in a container and bring the water to a boil with hot rocks. Add 1 cup of wild rice, cover the pot tightly, and allow the rice to steam.

Check the rice after 20 minutes. If the rice is not cooked, remove the rocks and add more hot rocks. Test again after ½ hour. The rice should be slightly chewy, with the grains separated.

Greens

The moist woodlands and meadows of the Pacific Northwest yield succulent greens today, just as they did long ago when Indian women gathered greens for part of their daily menu. Some of these plants rival our domestic garden varieties for flavor and texture, and may prove to be more nourishing. Some of the greens originated in European gardens and were brought to America by the colonists. These greens quickly spread in their new environment and reached the Pacific Northwest long before the first northwest settlers, and the Indians adopted the new plants into their diet.

Lamb's quarters or pig weed (*Chenopodium album*) — This modest plant, its flowers growing in a green spikelike cluster, possesses fleshy, angular toothed leaves which grow up to 4" long. They are excellent when picked young for both salad greens and as cooked vegetables. Indian cooks served them raw, with oolachan grease poured over them as dressing; or they tossed them into a pot of stew or soup, using the hot rocks method. The plant is an introduced variety.

Miner's lettuce or Indian lettuce (*Montia perfoliata*) — A delicious green, either raw or cooked, with a flavor somewhat like spinach, miner's lettuce served the early settlers just as it did the Indian cooks who preceded them. An annual, miner's lettuce grows up to 1' high from a small root stock. The basal leaves are ovate, with the upper leaves often united in pairs. The small, white flowers are found in loose clusters. Indians used this succulent plant as salad, using both the stems and the leaves, or they tossed it into the soup pot.

Clover *(Trifolium wormskjoldii)* — Purple clover was an important food plant for the people. Its tender new leaves were often mixed with other greens as a salad, or steamed and eaten with fish or seal oil. The root system was also used. The large taproot and horizontal rhizomic connectors were dug in the late fall or early spring in a manner similar to that used for camas. Both were prepared by steaming in pits until they were tender.

Sheep sorrel *(Rumer acetosella)* — Sheep sorrel is an inconspicuous plant that grows in dry, exposed fields. It is a perennial, rising on an erect stem from a fleshy root stock, reaching a height of up to one foot. It possesses greenish or reddish flowers in loose terminal clusters. Its leaves have a slightly sour taste which lend them to use as a seasoning in soups and sauces, and with other greens in salads. The plant is an introduced variety.

Glasswort *(Salicornia spp.)* — A one-of-a-kind plant, glasswort is easily found on wet tidal flats. It is perennial, fleshy, and leafless, with a juicy, jointed stem. In summer it is bright green and in the fall it turns red. This plant was valued by the Indians because of its high salt content. The stems made a salty salad, or added flavor to soups and stews. It was tender and made a good nibble food.

Cow parsnip or wild celery *(Heracleum lanatum)* — This giant among plants may reach 6' in height, with a massive flower head 4' to 10" across. Its leaves are equally large, arching from the thick main stem through a large sheath into 3 leaflets which may reach 3' in length. At the top, the main stalks divide into an umbrella of short stems, which branch again, supporting the flower heads. These heads are made up of hundreds of individual small white flowers. Cow parsnip is found growing in moist, rich soil from sea to subalpine areas.

Indians used the plant raw in salads. They peeled the flower stems before the flowers had opened and used the inner stems as we use raw celery. It was also cut into pieces and boiled until tender, as we do with celery.

Lamb's quarters
(Chenopodium album)

Miner's lettuce
(Montia perfoliata)

Clover
(Trifolium wormskjoldii)

Sheep sorrel
(Rumer acetosella)

Glasswort
(Salicornia spp.)

71

Cow parsnip
(Heracleum lanatum)

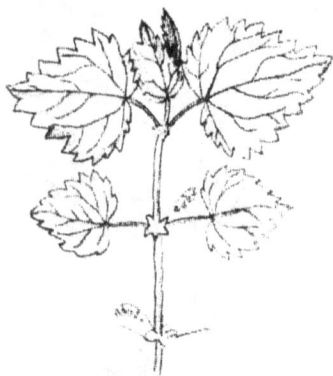

Nettle
(Urtica dioica)

Curlydock
(Rumer crispus)

Oyster plant
(Tragopogon porrifolius)

Cattail
(Typha latifolia)

Nettle *(Urtica dioica)* — The stinging nettle may not sound very appetizing, but once cooked, the sting is gone. The Indians used nettles for greens, boiling them in a pot using the hot rocks method. Nettles grow in shady places. Nettles should be picked early in the spring when they first emerge from the ground. Avoid the edge of the leaves when picking. The leaf edge contains the sting.

Oyster plant or salsify *(Tragopogon porrifolius)* — Salsify was introduced from Europe during the colonial days and spread across the continent. It was a favor for the Indians who adopted it into their diet. The young leaves were used for salads. The large, fleshy root was enjoyed as a potherb in soup. A bonus for the Indian children: the milky juice could be coagulated and chewed like gum.

Dock *(Rumer crispus, Rumer occidentalis, Arctium minus)* — One of the most useful plants available to the Indians, the three common varieties of dock—curlydock, yellow dock and burdock— were eaten as salad, boiled, smoked, and used as a meat tenderizer.

Young, tender dock leaves and stems were served with other greens as a vitamin-rich salad. Later in the season they were cooked with dandelion greens as potherbs. When dried, the leaves served as a tobacco. The plant was also used as a medicine and hair treatment.

Cattail *(Typha latifolia)* — Down inside of the cattail stock is a tender morsel, the heart of the plant. Strip away the reedlike leaves till you find the succulent interior. It may be eaten raw, sliced into salads, or cooked as a vegetable using the hot rocks method.

Salmonberry and thimbleberry *(Rubus spectabilis, Rubus parviflorus)* — When the tender new shoots grow on the salmonberry and thimbleberry bushes in early spring, break them off, peel away the tender skin, and eat as is. Indian children relished these shoots as today's children enjoy candy. Occasionally the Salish steamed the tender shoots and ate them as a vegetable.

Dandelion greens *(Taraxacum officinale)* — In the early spring the appearance of the hardy dandelion meant fresh salad and a welcome change from the heavy dried food of winter. The first tender green leaves were eaten raw with, perhaps, a dressing of fish oil. Later, the stronger, tougher leaves found their way into the soup pot. When the flower heads pushed up, the Indians chewed the rubbery stems as we would chew a stick of gum. The dandelion was introduced from Europe as a garden plant. It has adapted so well that we consider it a weed, and it was here waiting for the first settlers when they arrived on Puget Sound.

Fiddleheads *(Pteridium aquilinum, Athyrium filix-femina)* — The tender young shoots of bracken and lady fern, called fiddleheads, taste something like asparagus when cooked. They also make a tasty nibble food when eaten raw. The Coast Salish valued them as a spring tonic, for they are among the first greens to appear after a winter diet of dried food. The ferns were gathered while the "fiddlehead" was still tightly curled. After the wooly fuzz was rubbed from the stems, the women steamed the young ferns in pits or boiled them using the hot rocks method.

Berries

INDIAN WOMEN looked forward to the berry season with great anticipation. The fresh fruit provided badly needed vitamins and a delicious change in diet. As well, the women and girls gained an opportunity to get away by themselves for a picnicklike adventure.

Special berry baskets were woven during the winter months in anticipation of summer and the berry season. The women carried them on their backs with a tumpline across their foreheads holding them in place. This left the women's hands free to pick the berries.

Many berries were available including blackberries, blackcaps, huckleberries, blueberries, wild currants, salal, Oregon grape, and thimbleberries, but salmonberries seem to have been the favorite.

Salmonberry *(Rubus spectabilis)* — Salmonberries are a rather flavorless fruit that grow in moist areas of the forest. They can be identified by their orange to red berries that are about 1" in diameter. The berries are something like a raspberry. They ripen in early June. The bush grows up to 10' in height with scaling brown stems and very sparse thorns. Leaflets occur in threes. The 5-petaled flowers are red and over 1" in diameter. The berries were eaten fresh. The surplus was dried for the winter.

Small berry basket and carrying basket with strap

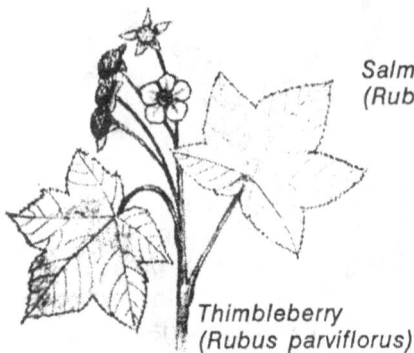

Salmonberry
(Rubus spectabilis)

Thimbleberry
(Rubus parviflorus)

Thimbleberry *(Rubus parviflorus)* — The dry, tasteless thimbleberry was not particularly relished, but since they were abundant, they were picked and dried for winter use along with other more favored fruits.

Thimbleberries bear soft, red, rounded berries, large maplelike leaves, and large white flowers. They grow in damp places on the fringe of forest openings. Berries ripen in July and August.

Huckleberry — Four species of huckleberry grow in the Pacific Northwest. All were prized by the Indian women.

The red huckleberry *(Vaccinium parvifolium)* is the most accessible, growing in the coastal forest below the 100-foot level. Old stumps are a favorite perch, and many a veteran cedar stump wears a crown of glossy leaves trimmed with red berries. The bushes grow to more than 6' high. They are compact with a mass of small oval leaves less than 1" long. Twigs and stems are as green as the leaves. Berries ripen in July.

The tall blue huckleberry *(Vaccinium ovalifolium)*, or whortleberry, is the tallest of the huckleberry family, sometimes reaching up to 8'. It favors shady locations in forests from sea level to subalpine regions. It bears pinkish bell blossoms which mature into berries that ripen in September. The tall blue huckleberry is rangy in shape due to its love of shade.

The black mountain huckleberry *(Vaccinium membranaceum)* or blue whortleberry is often known as the blueberry native to the high mountain meadows of the Pacific Northwest. This bush grows at an elevation of 2,500 feet or more, with its size changing with the elevation. It may reach 5' on the lower range, but becomes a dwarf of 1' or less at higher elevations. It bears a greenish white flower which gives birth to a smooth blue black berry of an excellent flavor. The berries ripen in September. The leaves, which grow from ½"

Tall blue huckleberry
(Vaccinium ovalifolium)

Red huckleberry
(Vaccinium parvifolium)

Black mountain huckleberry
(Vaccinium membranaceum)

Evergreen huckleberry
(Vaccinium ovatum)

to 1" in length, turn vivid shades of red in the late fall, giving the mountain meadows a touch of brilliant color.

The evergreen huckleberry *(Vaccinium ovatum)* bears small, shiny black berries of a sweet flavor. The berries ripen in October. The shrub is bushy and thick, rising crooked reddish limbs bearing fine-toothed leaves less than 1" long on very short stems. The plant's glossy leaves remain bright throughout the winter.

Salal *(Gaultheria shallon)* — Salal can be easily identified by its tough, evergreen, and somewhat egg-shaped leaves with pointed tips. Its pink flowers hang in a row from a stem like tiny bells. It bears dark blue berries that taste somewhat like blueberries. The berries ripen in August.

Indian cooks dried the berries and pressed them into cakes. In the winter the cakes were reconstituted by boiling them in water to make a syrup, or they were added to other food to improve the flavoring.

Soapberry, buffaloberry, russet buffaloberry, or soopolallie *(Shepherdia canadensis)* — A favorite of Indians wherever it grows, the soopolallie, which means soapberry, whips into a froth of foam, and is relished as a dessert. It grows into an upright bush up to 6' tall, or even taller in wooded areas. It is abundant in semiopen forests at medium elevations. The leaves are dark green with silvery hairs and rusty brown spots. Orange red, almost transparent berries of an elongated shape grow in small clusters along the stems and twigs. The berries are harvested in midsummer.

Soapberry
(Shepherdia canadensis)

Salal
(Gaultheria shallon)

The berries were placed in a wooden bowl and water was added, about three times the water as berry content. The berries were vigorously beaten until they foamed like egg whites and held a peak. Since the flavor of the soapberries is not nearly as delightful as their consistency, the Indians added oolachan grease. This was a real treat for them, and the old-timers speak in childhood memories of the occasions when soopolallies were served. Even today, Indian women pick the berries and whip them for their children. Today, most Indians will flavor soapberry foam with sugar.

Special hardwood paddles about 10" long were carved for whipping and eating the berries.

Wild strawberry (*Fragaria spp.*) — Wild strawberries are similar to their domestic cousins, but are about half the size. The plants are unique in that they have no stems. All the leaves and flowers grow individually from a scaly cluster attached above the roots. The flowers are white with 5 rounded petals, which ripen into ½" long berries in late June or early July. These delectable tidbits were eaten fresh as a treat. Children, particularly, enjoyed searching for them in open, sunny spaces.

Wild blackberry (*Rubus ursinus*) — The delicious fruit of the native blackberry grows in clusters along creeping vinelike stems that bristle with small thorns. The flowers are white, with five elongated petals and usually borne in small clusters. The berries, found in open, sunny areas, ripen in late July and early August. They were enjoyed fresh and the surplus was dried for winter.

78

Evergreen blackberry *(Rubus laciniatus)* — Introduced long ago by early settlers, the evergreen blackberry quickly became a staple in the Salish diet. The large berries with a sweet taste came as a great gift to the hardworking Indian women. The berries ripen in September. Berries were eaten fresh in great quantities, and the remainder of the harvest was dried along with other berries and processed into cakes. Today, both evergreen blackberries and Himalaya berries, which were introduced at a later date, are common along country roads and in open fields.

Wild strawberry   Evergreen blackberry   Wild blackberry
(Fragaria spp.)   (Rubus laciniatus)   (Rubus ursinus)

Black cap *(Rubus leucodermis)* — Resembling domesticated raspberries, black caps grow in clusters on long, arched, heavily thorned, greenish to purple branches in dry, open spaces. The flowers are white, while the berries mature to a dark, purplish black shade in late July and early August. Because of their high water content, they were usually eaten fresh. Leftover berries were dried and mixed with other berries.

Saskatoon or service berry *(Amelanchier alnifolia)* — Saskatoon is not actually a berry at all, but a fruit related to apples and pears. It grows on small trees and bears white blossoms early in the spring. Its fruit is very sweet, flavorful, and of firm consistency. It ripens in early August.

Indian cooks appreciated saskatoons because they dried well and were excellent for forming into cakes and storing for winter use.

Saskatoon berry
(Amelanchier alnifolia)

Black cap
(Rubus leucodermis)

Wild rose
(Rosa spp.)

Rose hips *(Rosa spp.)* — The berries of native roses, called rose hips, are rich in vitamin C. They are best gathered after the first frost, probably in October, when the skins have softened. The fruit may be eaten as is, utilizing just the pulpy material under the skin and leaving the seeds, which are large and hard. Rose hips were used by Indian women in their soups and stews.

Preparing berries for winter

Indian women developed food drying to a fine art. Today, the advantages of this type of food storage are becoming better recognized. A minimum of space is required in which to keep the food. With proper care, there is little danger of contamination and deterioration, and many valuable vitamins which are lost in cooking and freezing are preserved.

All berries could be dried for later use, but some were preferable, particularly those that possessed only a small amount of water and had a skin which held them together while they were drying. All the huckleberries, salal berries, saskatoon berries, and the Oregon grape fell into this category. Salmonberries, blackberries, and other soft berries were usually eaten when freshly picked, although a surplus could be processed provided there was sufficient hot sunshine to dry them adequately.

Indian women wove flat trays on which they laid the berries, placing them in the sun during the day and taking them inside at night to prevent any dew from moistening them again. Several times a day they would give the tray a flip to turn the berries so that they would dry evenly. When they were almost dry, they were pressed into cakes and cured in the sun or by smoking until completely dry. The pemmican-like substance was stored in airtight, covered baskets to keep moisture from ruining the berries during the cold, damp winter months.

For use, the berry cakes were broken into bits and reconstituted by the hot rocks method or eaten as is for a snack reminiscent of very hard, dry raisins. All the nutrition of sun-ripened berries was present in these cakes, and they provided that delightful change from the fish-oriented diet of winter.

Drying is equally valuable today, with shortages of canning supplies and the increasingly high cost of freezer facilities. The berries can be dried and stored without the final step of pressing into cakes, if desired. They can then be made into syrup, added to a mix for muffins or cakes, or be reconstituted and made into a fruit drink.

A window or door screen set outside in the sun on bricks makes a substitute for the woven tray. If flies are a problem, lay a piece of netting over the berries, or hang it just above them. Jiggle the screen several times a day to turn the berries. The length of time required to dry the berries will depend upon the heat of the sun. Take the screen inside at night to prevent dew from dampening the berries. When they are hard pellets, they are ready to store. It is possible to keep such berries for a year without deterioration.

A second method for drying the berries was also used by the Coast Salish of Puget Sound. The berries were sorted, destemmed and placed in cooking boxes where they were mashed until they were a juicy pulp. Hot rocks were then added to the juice and the berries were simmered until the juice thickened. When this jam was thick, it was poured into frames made of cedar bark and set on deveined skunk cabbage leaves. The frames were roughly several feet long and a foot wide by an inch deep. The filled frames were placed on racks over a low fire, near a fire, or in the sun, depending on conditions. After several days of drying, the berry cakes would be thick and rubbery. They were then folded or rolled and stored in boxes for the winter.

For use, the cakes were soaked in water overnight, mashed, and eaten with fish oil. They were also good eating as is, somewhat resembling our so-called berry leather, except that there were seeds present and the only sweetening was the natural fruit sugar.

Beverages

10

THE INDIANS of the Pacific Northwest enjoyed a variety of teas. Many of them were used because of their medicinal qualities, as well as for enjoyment.

Mint *(Mentha canadensis)* — Canada mint, and its relatives, provided a refreshing drink for Coast Salish Indians. Mint grew prolifically in damp lowlands, along stream banks, and by lakes. It has square stems, which may be covered with minute hairs, and small pointed leaves, which are evenly serrated. Tiny flowers bloom in July and August. They appear along the stems where the leaves join. The leaves were picked and dried in a shady place on baskets. To use, they were steeped in boiling water for several minutes.

Huckleberry — Wild huckleberry leaves were enjoyed as a tea. Branches were dried in the sun or hung in the rafters of the longhouses. The tiny leaves were stripped from the branches and brewed in hot water. This tea was considered to be a remedy for rheumatism.

Nettle *(Urtica dioica)* — Stinging nettle makes a good tea. Dry the nettles in a dark place on an openwork tray. When the leaves are dry, the sting is gone. Store the leaves in a tight container. Brew them as any tea.

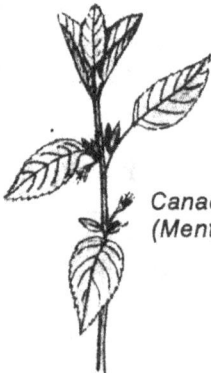

*Canada mint
(Mentha canadensis)*

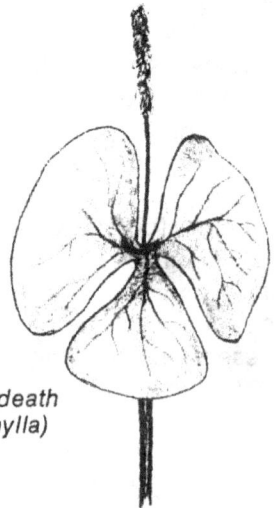

*Sweet after death
(Achlys triphylla)*

Madrona bark *(Arbutus menziesii)* — Madrona, or arbutus, is a beautiful tree which grows on Puget Sound islands and mainland shores. It has the unusual quality of retaining its waxy green leaves and shedding its red, paper bark. This gives a perpetual shaggy look to the tree. The bare skin of the trunk and limbs is satiny yellow green until it grows a new covering of reddish bark.

The Indians boiled the freshly peeled bark in water and drank it as a tea. It was also considered a remedy for diarrhea, for colds, and for bad coughs.

Wild cherry bark *(Prunus spp.)* — A tea made from wild cherry bark was used to cure a bad cough. The remedy is still used today. Indians are careful to point out that this is a strong drink, so be prepared for a taste out of the ordinary.

Peel the bark from the tree, steep it in boiling water for several minutes, and drink it as a tea. Wild cherry bark was also used as a healing agent for cuts and wounds. The Indians laid the bark on the affected area while the bark was still damp with sap.

Wild Blackberry and wild strawberry *(Rubus ursinus, Fragaria spp.)* — The leaves of these berry bushes make a light tea, reminiscent of Chinese jasmine tea. Gather the leaves about the first of June. Dry them in a dark place to keep the flavor and color. When the leaves are brittle, crush them and store them in a tight container.

To use, brew the leaves in boiling water for about 5 minutes. Serve with sugar if desired. The tea is also considered a remedy for diarrhea.

Sweet after death, elephant ear, or vanilla leaf *(Achlys triphylla)* — Sweet after death possesses aromatic qualities that were valued by pioneer women as an ingredient for sachets. It also makes a light, sweet beverage which was enjoyed by the Indians, particularly since sugar or other sweeteners were unavailable to them. The plant is easily identified by its 3 upright leaves, shaped like an elephant's ear, borne on a slender stem up to 1' in height. It occurs in shady, somewhat damp areas, often growing in colonies.

Dry the leaves in a dark place until they are papery thin and brittle. Store them in a tight container. To brew, place the leaves in a pan of cold water, bring them to a boil, and allow them to steep until the tea is of a strength that pleases your palate. There will be a slight vanilla taste to the tea.

Clover *(Trifolium spp.)* — All kinds of clover make good tea; however, the Yankee, or purple clover, seems to have been preferred by the Indians. It is a sweet tea with a refreshing flavor. Dry the blossoms and young leaves thoroughly and store them in a covered container. This is a delicate tea and it takes time to bring out the full flavor. Bring the clover to a boil in the water and allow it to steep for 10 minutes.

Tansy groundsel *(Senecio vulgarus)* — This plant makes an aromatic, refreshing drink. Indians claim that it was a cure for rheumatism.

Tansy is recognized by its feathery leaves and yellow flower head, like a daisy with no petals. It grows in dry areas to a height of about 1'. Pick the heads when they are in full bloom and dry them on a basket or screen surface in a dark area for about a week. Steep the leaves in boiling water for several minutes to brew them into a tea.

Indian tea or Oregon tea *(Satureja douglasii)* — Indian tea grows in low, somewhat damp areas, clinging to the ground, sometimes almost covered by grass or other plants. Its leaves are highly aromatic and slightly reminiscent of sage.

To prepare, bring the dried leaves to a boil in a pot of water. Remove it from the fire and allow it to steep until the flavor develops to your taste. Drink it as is, or with sugar and a dash of lemon.

The tea was also considered a valuable remedy for colds.

Berry punch — A sweet fruit drink was made from dried berries and honey. Wild honey was available to the Coast Salish Indians, and was utilized to sweeten berries for dessert, or in this delightful punch.

Drop a handful of dried berries into a pot of boiling water. Any kind or combination of berries will do. Allow the berries to simmer for half an hour. Strain the juice into another pot. Add the honey and heat just enough to blend the flavors. Drink it hot or allow it to cool. Stir the cooled drink to keep the honey in solution.

Indian tea
(Satureja douglasii)

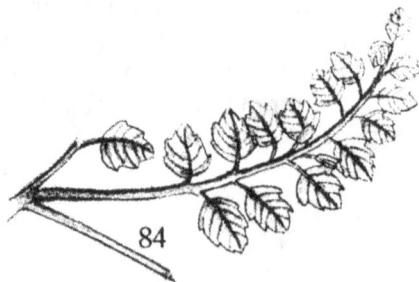

Condiments

11

Nodding Onion (*Allium cernuum*) — Nodding onion grows along the water's edge on dry slopes. A nodding, bent, onionlike flower of pink blooms grows on a 1' high stem. Grasslike leaves grow from the thin bulb. The bulb added flavor to soups and stews.

Iron wood or ocean spray leaves (*Holodiscus discolor*) — The small serrated leaves of the iron wood bush impart a delightful flavor to soups. The shrub usually grows in rocky places near the coast. It grows about 10' high and blooms with large cream flowers in large panicles from May to August.

Oolachan grease — Oolachan grease, a fish oil, was the Indian equivalent of butter, margarine, salad dressing, salad oil, and all other oily food we use to flavor, salve, and dress our food. It is a rich, nutritious oil that is pressed from the oolachan. This fish, a relative of smelt and hooligans, swarmed up the rivers of British Columbia in such numbers that they were captured by the thousands. The fish were tossed into pits and allowed to ripen for a week or more before the oil was pressed from them.

Oolachan oil has a strong taste which was appealing to the Northwest Indians in the past. It is still used and enjoyed by Indians

Iron wood
(*Halodiscus discolor*)

Nodding onion
(*Allium cernuum*)

today. It is an acquired taste which may not seem pleasing to un-educated palates.

Oolachan oil was used with dried berries in the winter as a dessert, as a dip for other dried food, and with reconstituted clams in chowder. In addition to its use as a highly valued condiment, oolachan oil was taken like cod liver oil as a remedy for colds. Indians heated the oil to luke warm and took the equivalent of 2 tablespoon-fuls every 2 hours.

While the Coast Salish did not have the great oolachan runs of their neighbors to the north, they did relish the fish oil and traded for it when possible. They produced it themselves in limited quan-tities.

Salmon egg oil — Fresh salmon eggs were placed in a bowl of wood or stone and ground with a mortar until they were a thick, oily mass, deliciously flavored of fish. This oil was used in the same manner as oolachan oil, when oolachan oil was not available.

The oil was of such high quality that it was also used as a base ingredient for paint. The paint lasted well, even on the outside walls of longhouses on rain-soaked Puget Sound.

Other oils — When oolachan grease was not available, the Coast Salish people turned to other sources. Bear fat and seal oil were saved from the dripping meat during the barbecue process or were skimmed from cooking baskets or boxes.

There are some reports that indicate bear fat was stored in coils of cleaned intestines. The fat hardened into a tube shape when cooled. Seal and dogfish oil were stored in seal stomachs. The stomach was removed from the seal, turned inside out, inflated, and dried. Softened with oil, it made a convenient storage container. Wooden chests were also used for grease and oil storage. Some-times the oil was poured into cured hollow kelp bulbs and stems before being stored in boxes.

Dried herring eggs — Herring eggs were added to simmering food as a special treat. They cooked to a tender, jellylike consistency and added excitement to a mundane stew.

Seaweed — It is difficult to know whether to consider seaweed a vegetable or a seasoning agent. It was relished both fresh and dried for its salty savor and for its taste. Added to soups and stews, it gave a special zing that tickled the Indian palate. Eaten dried, it was the Salish version of potato chips. Nibbled fresh, it was a perfectly acceptable salad green.

Several varieties of seaweed were utilized. The green sea lettuce *(Ulva spp.)*, so prized by Japanese and Hawaiians, was also enjoyed by coastal Indians. It is deliciously salty and tender. When spread in the sun to dry, it took on a tender-crisp consistency. It was dried thoroughly and layered into cakes in airtight containers for winter use.

A black seaweed called dulce *(Fucus spp.)* was found on rocks at low tide near open water. It was generally dried on the rocks in the summer sun and stored for winter use in boiled food. Even today, Indians gather it. They sometimes go great distances to seek it in open seawater. It is particularly enjoyed when eaten dried as a snack.

Kelp bulbs *(Nereocystis leutkeana)* were utilized as an addition to stews. They were used in the fresh state. Only bulbs of good quality were cooked. These were chopped and added to pot-boiled food.

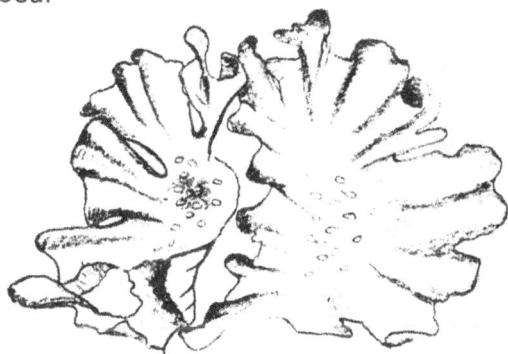

Sea lettuce
(Ulva spp.)

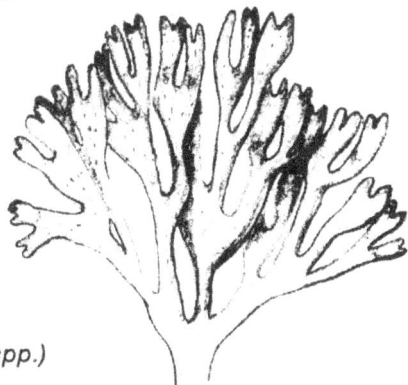

Dulce
(Fucus spp.)

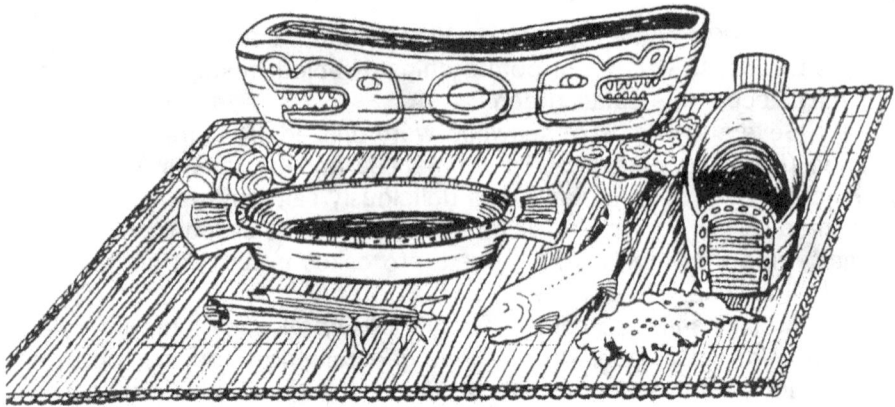

Come to the Feast

Winter comes to the Coast Salish territory along the inlets of Puget Sound. The people return from their quest for food to permanent villages which crouch on high ground just beyond the beaches. There is time for leisure now, and for making necessities such as baskets, mats, nets, lures, and weapons. There is time, too, for those things which are important to the Salish culture: stories and ceremonies, songs and dances, and feasting.

Life in the great longhouses assumes a relaxed routine which is a welcome change from the food gathering expeditions which have dominated the days since last spring. Outside, rain pelts the heavy cedar wall boards, hewn from a living tree or wedged out from a fallen tree and adzed to evenness. Occasionally a drop falls through one of the smoke holes and sizzles as it hits the glowing coals of the fires below. Near the fire it is warm and cozy, but toward the door and along the walls there is a feeling of damp chill in spite of the heavy matting of woven cattails that lines the interior. Storage boxes and baskets are stacked on shelves that range along the walls above each family's sleeping compartment. It has been a good year and there is enough food to last until spring, with a surplus to share with friends.

In his extravagantly large house, the old chief of one of the many Salish groups sits in thoughtful silence. He watches the activities of his family from his vantage point on a platform at the far end of the room. Here live his several wives and their now-grown sons who, together with their own wives and offspring, have added to the expanding population of the great house. There are nephews, too, who have contributed to the throng of little ones playing on the spacious dirt floor. The elderly man surveys the scene with great satisfaction.

The family has been up and about for several hours. In spite of the rain and cold, they have gone to the river to bathe. Now the women sweep the hard-packed earthen floor around the firepits. They fan the embers from yesterday's fire into flame and add cedar twigs and bits of cedar bark. When the flames are leaping merrily, the women lay cooking stones alongside to heat.

The chief watches as some of the younger women enter with wooden water buckets freshly filled from the river. He smiles with anticipation as the women take down storage boxes and bring out the food that they plan to cook for the day. He always has a good feeling when plenty of food has been put away. He remembers the gnawing ache of an empty belly. This year everyone will eat well. "Perhaps," he thinks, "it is time to give a feast."

He watches his first wife, the head wife and matriarch of the tribe, lift a smoked salmon from the soaking box where she had placed it the night before. Placing it on a cedar board, she pounds it until the flesh is soft, picking out any bones that lurk in the flesh. She places it in a watertight cooking basket and tosses in a chunk of dried seaweed to give it extra savor and to thicken the broth. She sprinkles water on the cooking rocks. When they sizzle, she picks them up with tongs and drops them into the basket. Steam rises and the old chief inhales the delectable aroma.

The woman lays a cattail mat on the floor near her firepit. She places a wooden serving tray of fish upon it. The fish is tender and smells deliciously of smoke. Individual wooden spoons are placed on the mat. When all is ready, the old man descends from his place and joins his family. It is he who takes the first taste. Only then do the others join in. They eat in silence, enjoying the taste and texture of the food.

After his meal the old man rises stiffly from the floor and returns to his seat. He brings out his pipe to enjoy a smoke, stuffs dried kinnikinnick into the bowl of hollowed stone, and draws thoughtfully through the hollow-reed stem. In the spring, while walking the trails, he had gathered the leaves of the trailing kinnikinnick, along with alder bark and salal leaves. Now, in the long winter day, he can enjoy a pipe filled with the makings.

After some time he reaches for his *talking stick* and raps it sharply on the wooden platform. Instantly, the activity in the house stops and everyone looks his way, waiting to hear what he has to say.

"It is time for us to give a feast. We have much food. The season of ceremonials is upon us. We will send out *cous* 'invitation' to the great families in the nearby villages. We will invite them to come in twenty suns. My nephews will carry the invitation sticks."

There is a murmur of excitement among the women. Their thoughts are concerned with practical matters. There is much to do and so little time to do it. They will be expected to serve meals to a hundred or more people for several days. Maybe their guests will remain even longer, for it would be unthinkable to limit their stay. There is plenty of food, but this is only part of it. Everything must be in order and in readiness. Are there enough mats? Or must more be made? They will need a great supply of shredded cedar bark for napkins. The old women and girls can work on that. Are the wooden serving dishes in good repair? Will the men find time to repair them or make new ones? The matriarch looks at the other women who are gathered around her. She nods and they smile back. It will be a busy time, these next twenty days.

The young men, too, nod their approval. There will be the excitement of the *sla hal* game, with the chance to gain wealth or to lose what one already has. They will dance their spirit dances and feel the great power of their spirit gifts come upon them. The men have concerns, too. Is the dance paraphernalia in good condition? Are the dance costumes, masks, and drums in readiness? Their own personal prestige, as well as the family's, depends on the perfection of their appearance and skill when performing. There is much to be considered. If all is not done correctly everyone will suffer humiliation. Their guests will depart only to ridicule them, and soon word would pass among the villages that the chief and his house did not know how to give a great feast. The men turn their minds and efforts to the ceremonial aspects of the gathering, looking to the old man for counsel and guidance.

After days of preparation, the time of the feast comes. Dressed in their fur robes and cedar-bark headdress, the chief and elders of the family watch eagerly for the first sign of canoes bringing guests from the other villages. Drums and sticks are ready to beat out the welcome song. Anklets of rattling deer hooves are ready to be tied around the ankles of the dancers.

Suddenly the bay is filled with canoes. Across the water the chanting of songs is heard as the paddlers bring their craft nearer. Inside the longhouse, all is ready. The women and girls have quickly taken their places for the welcome dance, which is theirs alone to perform.

When the guests have assembled in the great house, the old chief mounts his platform at the end of the room opposite the low door and raps sharply with his stick. Instantly there is silence as everyone gives him full attention.

"Welcome to my house," he begins, his voice booming out the words. "You will see that our hospitality is the greatest of all and our food beyond compare. You will see the great power of our songs and dances." He raps his stick and motions to the women to begin their welcome dance. Seated below his platform, the drummers begin the beat, softly at first and then louder as they feel the rhythm. Slowly the women begin to move and sing. Arms outstretched in a gesture of welcome, moving to the right and to the left to include each guest, they serpentine through the crowd, making their way around the fires, past the chief, and back to the opposite end of the house.

The chief again raps for attention. "You must be hungry, for you have come from far away," he says. "We have much food, which our women have prepared for you. Come and sit in the places I have reserved for you."

The old man proceeds to seat each guest according to his rank and importance, in the time-honored custom of the people. The most important guests are given places of honor at his side. Others are ranged along the sides of the longhouse while those of least consequence must be content near the door with its drafts of cold air.

"Let the feast begin," the old man commands, emphasizing his words by banging his talking stick on the platform floor. At the signal, the women bring ladles and wooden buckets filled with freshly drawn water. These are offered to the guests so that they may rinse their mouths to refresh and cleanse them in anticipation of the food to come. Then towels of cedar bark, pounded soft and thin like paper, are given to the guests so that they may wipe surface grime from their hands. Next, according to the custom of high caste families, wooden boxes filled with water are carried to the guests so that they can rinse their hands. More shredded bark towels are offered.

The cleansing ritual accomplished, the women and their helpers again pass buckets of water and ladles to their guests. This time the water is to drink. It is the only water that will be offered until the feast is over, for it is considered bad manners to drink while eating. Each guest is careful to drink sparingly, indicating that he is not really hungry and is not greatly impressed by his host's boast of prosperity.

The girls lay out the cattail mats on which to place the food. They carefully lay wooden eating ladles before each guest. It is the custom to eat from common trays, but it must be done delicately with individual spoons.

The heat in the house is building to the point where it is uncomfortable. The leaping fires threaten to scorch the mats, but no one seems to notice. At intervals one of the chief's slaves pours fish oil on the flames to fan them higher, increasing their intensity until they threaten to burn the rafters. Still, the guests seem not to notice. It is customary for the host to impress his guests by pouring valuable oil on the fire, but the guests must not show that they are impressed.

A first course of dried fish is placed in trays on the mats before the diners. Side dishes of fish and seal oil are included. The guests are invited to nibble on these appetizers while the more substantial food is being served. Using their fingers, the diners delicately dip the pieces of hard, smoked fish in the bowls of oil and slip them in their mouths, being careful not to show their teeth. When the guests are finished, the girls again pass water boxes and cedar bark towels. The women bring huge carved trays filled with steaming soup made from the broth and meat of ducks, thickened with dried seaweed and seasoned with camas. The guests gather about the trays, sipping from the tip of their ladles. The assemblage eats quietly with downcast eyes.

Handsomely carved containers are placed on the mats. Steaming hot, boiled dried salmon cooked to a soft consistency fills the three-foot-long dishes. Side dishes of fish oil round out the course. Using their fingers, the feasters eat slowly, savoring each mouthful.

Next on the menu comes dried berries. These are served in wafer form, with the ever-present accompaniment of fish oil in which to dip them. When the guests have had their fill, more water and towels for hand rinsing are passed.

As a final offering and special treat, wooden bowls of frothy, whipped soapberries are placed on the mats. The women give each guest a small wooden paddle and they dip the foamy concoction from the central bowls. The guests almost forget their decorum when this favorite treat is placed before them. The old chief watches his guests from the vantage point of the platform. He notices their enthusiasm and suddenly realizes that his feast is a success.

There has been no conversation. It has been a time for eating, and for enjoying. Eyes have been lowered to enjoy the sight of the food. The eating has been done quietly, since mouth noises are considered to be rude. No one has hurried. Food takes time – gathering, drying, storing, preparation – and it must be eaten with a feeling of appreciation.

Now the meal is finished. Finger bowls of warm water and more towels are passed. At last, the drinking buckets and ladle make their rounds. Again, the guests are careful not to drink too much, for that would be a sign that they have overeaten.

The chief rises from his chair, hits the floor sharply with his talking stick and says: "You have seen that my boast was not an idle one. You have eaten well. You will long remember my hospitality. You will say, 'He scorched my clothes with the heat of his fire. He poured oil on the fire for he has an abundance. He gave us more food than we could eat. He is a great and powerful man.' I call upon witnesses to say that this is true, and to tell all the people of the feast that I gave."

According to accepted custom, several of those who have been honored by seats at the head of the house rise and agree. "I will witness for you. Your hospitality is beyond reproach," each says in turn. "Your name will be known and spoken with respect for you have great abundance and you share it with others."

The feast is over. For three days the longhouse has echoed with the beat of drums, the songs of the *sla hal* game, the excitement of the spirit dances, and the great songs, repeated for all to hear. Now it is quiet.

The old man feels suddenly very cold and very old. His great house is dark. Only a small fire glows where yesterday there was such a fire that it threatened to char the great roof supports. His family sits by the small flame. They are tired, too tired to think of food now. Indeed, it is all the women have thought of for these last days.

Many of the food baskets are empty. The chief's overabundance is gone. There will be barely enough food to last until the ducks fly again and the salmon people come swarming from their undersea villages. The chief smiles and his face lights with the glory of it all. "I am a great man," he says to himself. "I have given a great feast. Everyone has said so. I and my family are a great family."

Soon it all will begin again. Soon the people will make new nets, new fishing gear, and new baskets. Spring plans must be made. Soon they will gather more food. The yearly cycle will begin again.

Further Reading

Ashwell, Reg. *Coast Salish: Their Art, Culture and Legends.* Surrey, B.C.: Hancock House Publishers, 1978.

Domico, Terry. *Wild Harvest: Edible Plants of the Pacific Northwest.* Surrey, B.C.: Hancock House Publishers, 1979.

Gunther, Erna. *Ethno-Botany of Western Washington.* Seattle: University of Washington Press, 1945.

Gunther, Erna. *Indian Life on the Northwest Coast of North America.* Chicago: University of Chicago Press, 1972.

Harbo, Rick M. *The Edible Seashore: Pacific Shores Cookbook & Guide.* Surrey, B.C.: Hancock House Publishers, 1988.

Harbo, Rick M. *Guide to the Western Seashore.* Surrey, B.C.: Hancock House Publishers, 1988.

Harbo, Rick M. *Tidepool & Reef: Marinelife Guide to the Pacific Northwest Coast.* Surrey, B.C.: Hancock House Publishers, 1980.

Lyons, C. P. *Trees, Shrubs and Flowers to Know in Washington.* Toronto: J. M. Dent and Sons, 1952.

Stark, Raymond. *Guide to Indian Herbs.* Surrey, B.C.: Hancock House Publishers, 1981.

Thompson, Mary, and Thompson, Steven. *Huckleberry Country: Wild Food Plants of the Pacific Northwest.* Berkeley: Wilderness Press, 1977.

Turner, Nancy. *Food Plants of British Columbia Indians, Part I: Coast Peoples.* Victoria, B.C.: British Columbia Provincial Museum, 1975.

Underhill, J. E. (Ted). *Northwest Wild Berries.* Surrey, B.C.: Hancock House Publishers, 1980.

Underhill, Ruth. *Indians of the Pacific Northwest.* Washington D.C.: Bureau of Indian Affairs, 1945.

Metric Conversion Chart

½ inch	12.5 millimeters
1 inch	2.5 centimeters
1 foot	30 centimeters
1 foot	0.30 meter
1 pound	0.50 kilogram
1 cup (8 oz.)	250 milliliters

(approximations)

Index

Other Hancock House Books

WESTERN NATURE TITLES

Edible Seashore (cookbook & guide)
Rick M. Harbo
ISBN 0-88839-199-4

Exploring the Ourdoors: SW B.C.
Tony Eberts & Al Grass
ISBN 0-88839-989-8

Guide to the Western Seashore
Rick M. Harbo
ISBN 0-88839-201-X

How to Catch Really Big Fish
Tara Robinson
ISBN 0-88839-967-7

NW Wild Berries
J. E. (Ted) Underhill
ISBN 0-88839-027-0

Wild Harvest: Edible Plants of the NW
Terry Domico
ISBN 0-88839-022-X

Our Underwater World
Joe Liburdi & Harry Truitt
ISBN 0-919654-00-2

Pacific Wilderness
David Hancock, Lyn Hancock & David Sterling
ISBN 0-919654-08-8

Rafting in British Columbia
Doug VanDine & Bernard Fandrich
ISBN 0-88839-985-5

Rocks & Minerals of the NW
Stan Leaming & Chris Leaming
ISBN 0-88839-053-X

Tidepool & Reef
Rick M. Harbo
ISBN 0-88839-039-4

Wildflowers Series

    Alpine Wildflowers
    J. E. (Ted) Underhill
    ISBN 0-88839-975-8

    Coastal Lowland Wildflowers
    J. E. (Ted) Underhill
    ISBN 0-88839-973-1

    NW Roadside Wildflowers
    J. E. (Ted) Underhill
    ISBN 0-88839-108-0

    Sagebrush Wildflowers
    J. E. (Ted) Underhill
    ISBN 0-88839-171-4

    Upland Field & Forest Wildflowers
    J. E. (Ted) Underhill
    ISBN 0-88839-174-9

Western Mushrooms
J. E. (Ted) Underhill
ISBN 0-88839-031-9

Western Wildlife
David Hancock
ISBN 0-919654-81-9

Wildlife of the Rockies
David Hancock
Photos: Tom W. Hall
ISBN 0-919654-33-9

INDIAN TITLES

Ah Mo
Tren Griffin
ISBN 0-88839-244-3

American Indian Pottery
Sharon Wirt
ISBN 0-88839-134-X

Argillite: Art of the Haida
Leslie Drew & Douglas Wilson
ISBN 0-88839-037-8

Art & Style of Western Indian Basketry
Joan Megan Jones, PhD
ISBN 0-88839-122-6

Art of the Totem
Marius Barbeau
ISBN 0-88839-168-4

Artifacts of the NW Coast Indians
Hilary Stewart
ISBN 0-88839-098-X

Blackfeet
John C. Ewers
ISBN 0-88839-170-6

Coast Salish
Reg Ashwell
ISBN 0-88839-009-2

Guide to Indian Quillworking
Christy Ann Hensler
ISBN 0-88839-214-1

Haida: Their Art & Culture
Leslie Drew
ISBN 0-88839-132-3

Hunter Series
By R. Stephen Irwin, MD,
Illustrations by J. B. Clemens:

    Hunters of the Buffalo
    ISBN 0-88839-176-5

    Hunters of the Eastern Forest
    ISBN 0-88839-178-1

    Hunters of the Ice
    ISBN 0-88839-179-X

    Hunters of the Northern Forest
    ISBN 0-88839-175-7

    Hunters of the Sea
    ISBN 0-88839-177-3

Images: Stone: B.C.
Wilson Duff
ISBN 0-295-95421-3

Indian Art & Culture
Della Kew & P. E. Goddard
ISBN 0-919654-13-4

Indian Artifacts of the NE
Roger W. Moeller
ISBN 0-88839-127-7

Indian Coloring Books
Carol Batdorf

    Gifts of the Seasons
    Drawings by Katheryn Graves
    ISBN 0-88839-246-X

    Seawolf
    Drawings by Pat Clark
    ISBN 0-88839-247-8

Tinka
Drawings by Carol Batdorf
ISBN 0-88839-249-4

Totem Poles
Drawings by Tracy Cheney
ISBN 0-88839-248-6

Indian Healing
Wolfgang G. Jilek, MD
ISBN 0-88839-120-X

Indian Herbs
Dr. Raymond Stark
ISBN 0-88839-077-7

Indian Rock Carvings of the Pacific NW Coast
Beth Hill
ISBN 0-919654-34-7

Indian Tribes of the NW
Reg Ashwell
ISBN 0-919654-53-3

Indian Weaving, Knitting & Basketry of the NW
Elizabeth Hawkins
ISBN 0-88839-006-8

Indians of the NW Coast
D. Allen
ISBN 0-919654-82-7

Iroquois: Their Art & Crafts
Carrie A. Lyford
ISBN 0-88839-135-8

Kwakiutl Legends
Chief James Wallas & Pamela Whitaker
ISBN 0-88839-094-7

My Heart Soars
Chief Dan George
Drawings by Helmut Hirnschall
ISBN 0-88839-231-1

My Spirit Soars
Chief Dan George
& Helmut Hirnschall
ISBN 0-88839-233-8

North American Indians
Mike Roberts
ISBN 0-88839-000-9

Northwest Native Harvest
Carol Batdorf
ISBN 0-88839-245-1

The Providers
R. Stephen Irwin, MD
ISBN 0-88839-181-1

The Song of Creation
Helmut Hirnschall
ISBN 0-920882-06-4

Spirit Quest
Carol Batdorf
ISBN 0-88839-210-9

Those Born at Koona
John & Carolyn Smyly
ISBN 0-88839-101-3

Tlingit: Their Art, Culture & Legends
Dan & Nan Kaiper
ISBN 0-88839-010-6

Totem Poles of the NW
D. Allen
ISBN 0-919654-83-5

other native culture titles from HANCOCK HOUSE PUBLISHERS

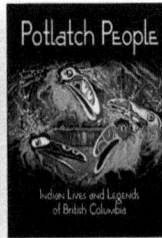

Hancock House Publishers
19313 0 Ave, Surrey, BC V3Z 9R9
www.hancockhouse.com
sales@hancockhouse.com
1-800-938-1114